America's Bubble Economy

America's Bubble Economy

Profit When It Pops

John David Wiedemer, PhD
Robert A. Wiedemer
and
Cindy S. Spitzer

With a Chapter on Gold
for People who Hate Gold
by
Eric Janszen

WILEY

John Wiley & Sons, Inc.

Published by John Wiley & Sons, Inc., Hoboken, New Jersey.

Published simultaneously in Canada.

For general information on our other products and services or for technical support, please contact our Customer Care Department within the United States at (800) 762–2974, outside the United States at (317) 572–3993 or fax (317) 572–4002.

Wiley also publishes its books in a variety of electronic formats. Some content that appears in print may not be available in electronic books. For more information about Wiley products, visit our web site at www.wiley.com.

Library of Congress Cataloging-in-Publication Data:

Wiedemer, John David.
    America's bubble economy : profit when it pops / John David Wiedemer, Robert A. Wiedemer, and Cindy S. Spitzer.
        p. cm.
    Includes index.
    ISBN-13: 978–0–471-75367-4 (cloth)
    ISBN-10: 0–471-75367-X (cloth)
    1. Financial crises—United States.   2. Debt—United States.   3. United States—Economic conditions—2001–   4. Finance, Personal—United States.   5. Asset allocation—United States.   I. Wiedemer, Robert A.   II. Spitzer, Cindy S.   III. Title.
    HB3722.W53 2006
    332.02400973—dc22   2006013380

Printed in the United States of America.

10 9 8 7 6 5 4 3 2 1

Contents

Acknowledgments

The authors thank **John Silbersack** of Trident Media Group and Wiley editor **David Pugh** for supporting this unique project. Our gratitude also goes to **John Douglas**, our "in-house" editor, whose early guidance and on-going support led us to publication, to **Eric Janszen** for his "golden" insights and fresh thinking, to our illustrator **Tim Kestel** for helping us make grim finances more understandable, and to **David Robbinette** and **Jennis Taylor** for their research assistance.

David Wiedemer

I thank my co-authors Bob and Cindy for being indispensable in the writing of this book. Without them this book would not have been published and if written, inaccessible for most audiences. I also thank Dr. Rod Stevenson for his long-term support of the foundation work that is the basis for this book, which hopefully will be the first of many. And I am especially grateful to my wife Betsy and son

Benson for their on-going support in what has been an often arduous and trying process.

Bob Wiedemer

I thank Ron Everett, my business associate, for his enthusiastic support of this project, my brother Jim for his lifelong support of the ideas behind this book, my father, a lifelong author, and my mother for inspiring me with the joy of discovering the world and writing about it. I am also grateful to Weldon Rackley, Steve Schnipper, Phil Gross, and David Boelio for their early support that made all the difference, and to our review group, Greg Karmazin, Greg Pearl, Bill Clark, and Dr. Rod Stevenson, for their feedback throughout this long process.

Thank you, Tim Miller for your generosity in helping me, and Tony Perkins for introducing me to Eric Janszen.

Of course, my gratitude goes to Dave Wiedemer and Cindy Spitzer for being quite clearly, the best collaborators you could ever have. It was truly a great team effort. Most of all, I thank my wife Sera, and children, Seline and John, without whose love and support, this book, and a really great life, would not be possible.

Cindy Spitzer

Thank you, David and Bob, for trusting me with this exciting project and for letting me in, early, on one of the biggest, most important secrets of our time. My love and gratitude go to my wonderful husband Philip Terbush and precious children Chelsea, Zachary, and almost-daughter

Acknowledgments

Anya; to my recently departed dear friends Marian Sharif and Cynthia Carter; to my gifted mentor, two-time Pulitzer Prize winner Jon Franklin, whom I haven't seen in almost two decades but still learn from daily; to my brilliant brothers Scott and Skip Spitzer, and to my ever-effervescent parents Stan and Rose Spitzer for somehow giving me the impression that anything is possible.

Introduction

Remember the Internet Stock Bubble? It was big. It was bold. It was going to drive the "New Economy" into the new millennium.

Then it popped.

Hindsight, of course, is 20/20. But back in those glory days of the roaring 1990s, it looked like the sky was the limit. In reality, the limit turned out to be a lot closer to the ground. Despite all the hype and wishful thinking, the overinflated Internet Bubble—like every bubble before and since—was subject to the same laws of gravity that apply to the rest of the economy. Without real underlying growth, without real profits and productivity gains, sooner or later, *what goes up must come down*.

While fortunes were lost and dozens of high-tech companies went belly up, the popping of the relatively small Internet Bubble was merely a sneak preview of the financial earthquake that is yet to come. Rumbling ominously beneath our seemingly prosperous economy are not one, but several linked financial bubbles that are threatening to interact, collide, and ultimately pop.

Together, the bursting of America's bubble economy will create a temporary Bubblequake of shockwaves here and around the world, depressing stock and real estate values, driving up interest rates and inflation, and throwing the U.S. and other economies into temporary global recession.

The good news is the coming Bubblequake won't last forever and will help transform our international monetary system and economy both here and abroad.

And the really good news is that *you* can cash in on it in a big way—*if* you see it coming.

A Word to the Wise

We understand that smart, reasonable people don't buy every new idea that comes down the pike. All we ask is that you keep an open mind and hear us out. Certainly, we can all agree that our current economy faces some real challenges:

- Huge international trade deficits that just keep getting bigger.

- An astronomical $8 trillion federal government debt, heavily financed by foreign capital.

- Ever-expanding consumer debt with no equal rise in consumer income

- The lowest savings rates in our nation's history.

- A national housing market that has climbed 80 percent in the last 5 years, while incomes rose only 2 percent.

- An economy that's now heavily dependent on historically low interest rates and low inflation rates that require massive foreign capital to maintain.

Clearly, the current situation is far from ideal. We don't expect everyone to agree with our entire analysis of how we got here and what's ahead, but we do hope to give something valuable to anyone who, like us, believes that current conditions are simply not sustainable. We hope to give you a logical basis for rational actions that can help you prevent significant asset loss and perhaps even create tremendous wealth when the current conditions can no longer be sustained.

Whether or not you buy all the ideas in this book, it will give you a new way to think about how the above problems developed and where they might be headed next. Even more valuable, the book offers fresh insights about how these conditions may directly impact you and what specific steps you can take to protect your assets and even cash in on it. Please don't blow this golden opportunity by quibbling over the debatable details. You needn't believe all we say to position yourself right now to make huge profits in the very near future.

A Word to the Easily Bored

This is not your father's finance book. Yes, we rely on solid economics not only because one of the authors is an evolutionary economist, but because it is the only reliable way to understand what is happening now and will happen next in the financial world. But rest assured, we will not numb you with numbers. Instead of drowning you in details, we've boiled it all down to the most essential insights you need to come to your own conclusions about the coming bubble trouble. Even if you never read a book about economics or finances before, you simply cannot afford to miss this one. Give us a chance and we promise not to put you asleep.

A Word to the Perpetually Busy

If you don't have time to read this entire book, we understand because we really didn't have time to write it. Of course, we'd love it if you read the whole thing and told all your friends to do the same. But if you only have time for the essentials, here's how to get the most out of reading the least, based on your particular interests:

- If you just want the basics about *America's Bubble Economy*, simply read Chapter 1, your "Executive Summary."

- For a deeper understanding of how the greatest economy on the planet managed to deny its way into this mess, proceed to Chapter 2, "Bubble Blind."

- If you'd like more details about when the bubbles pop, and you think our logic is either right on target or way off the mark, please check out Chapter 3, "Bubble-quake: A Likely Scenario," and Chapter 4, "What!? You Mean We're Not the King of the World!?"

- Everyone who wants to protect their assets and make huge profits when the bubbles burst (no matter what your current wealth level), will find priceless news-you-can-use in Chapter 5, "Cashing in on Chaos," and Chapter 6, "Gold for People Who Hate Gold." The gold chapter, by the way, is written by financial bubble expert Eric Janszen. The insider insights don't get any better than this.

- If you have a business to grow, or any hope of getting and keeping a job in the very different post-bubble economy, check out Chapter 7, "Survive and Thrive."

- And finally, for all our fellow "Big Picture" thinkers, we offer something truly unique and thoroughly mind-stretching: An entirely new way to see how this particular slice of history fits into the broader evolution of money and the even broader evolution of society itself. We can't wait to hear what you think of Chapter 8, "The View From 30,000 Feet." No matter how this outlook grabs you, we promise you won't find a *bigger* Big Picture anywhere else.

For more information than we could possibly fit in the book and for the most recent developments and indicators on the financial bubbles, how we created them, and what will happen when they pop, please visit the book's web site at **www.americasbubbleeconomy.com.** Throughout the book, we give you specific links to specific areas of our web site, so you don't have to search the entire site to find what you need. For example, to contact the authors or offer feedback on the book, please visit **www.americasbubbleeconomy.com/comments.**

John David Wiedemer
Robert A. Wiedemer
Cindy S. Spitzer

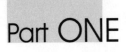

Part ONE

AMERICA'S BUBBLE ECONOMY

Chapter ONE

Executive Summary

Do We Really Have a Bubble Economy and Why Should I Care?

If the idea that a cluster of dangerous financial bubbles now threatens the United States and other world economies seems pretty outlandish to you, you are not alone. Conventional wisdom says the United States has and always will be the greatest economy the world has ever known, and there's no reason to believe the pessimistic naysayers and the perpetually paranoid chicken-littles who keep insisting the sky is falling.

But what if there were a smarter, more realistic way to look at it? What if you didn't have to be blinded by wishful thinking nor consumed with fears of impending doom and gloom? What if you could see the factual evidence for yourself, come to your own reasonable conclusions, and prepare now to be among the wise few who will capitalize on what others initially miss?

While most people will continue to ignore the warning signs until it's too late, smart, reasonable people can figure out how to survive and thrive under any conditions.

The key is to face the facts early, use common sense, and act quickly and correctly.

Facing Facts

Let's begin with what most smart, reasonable people can agree on: Despite some recent gains, the current U.S. economy is sluggish and now faces some potentially significant destabilizing factors.

For starters, we now have the biggest international *trade deficit* and domestic *budget deficit* in our nation's history. We also have record-breaking *consumer debt*, coupled with a *near-zero savings rate*. In many sectors, new jobs are not being created as fast as they used to be. Unemployment is creeping up in some regions, and many people who do have jobs haven't seen a decent raise in years.

So, the first fact we face is that on every level of our economy—from overextended families to overextended businesses to overextended state and national governments—there is often more money going out than there is coming in.

In and of itself, this doesn't necessarily mean we're in trouble. After all, a medical student might be in debt up to her eyeballs with no income to speak of and later go on to pay off all her loans and enjoy a very prosperous financial life. The same is true of national economies. Debt coupled with low income is not necessarily a bad thing. Like the medical student, governments can use debt as a tool to greatly increase prosperity down the road. It all depends on future potential.

Which brings us to the next set of facts we face. What

exactly is our economy's future potential based on what we know about present conditions?

No one can say with certainty what tomorrow will bring, but reasonable people, given accurate information, can come to their own reasonable conclusions. Again, let's look at a few telling facts. We know we have a *booming housing market* that can't expand forever. We have a *volatile stock market* that climbs and falls as skittish investors dash in and out. We have a *declining dollar* that countries, such as China and Japan, may grow leery of

"Tell me the fairytale about the economy."

buying in huge quantities. And even more pressing, we have a national economy that is heavily dependent on unprecedented low interest rates and low inflation rates that simply cannot last forever.

Clearly, everything is not exactly coming up roses. But can we reasonably jump from these current realities to the conclusion that we have several linked bubbles that are about to simultaneously burst, sending a shockwave of troubles through the entire global economy?

Most people would say no. But then, most people have never peeled back the skin of a bubble. Come inside and see for yourself . . .

What Is a Bubble?

There is no formal definition within the field of economics that provides a precise way of identifying a bubble. For our purposes, we say a bubble exists whenever an asset's *perceived or psychological value* exceeds its real *economic value*. By economic value, we mean a value that is based on logical economic parameters, such as population growth, rising company earnings, increased personal income, or some other fundamental economic parameter that is directly tied to the asset's rise in value. On the other hand, if the asset begins to sell for a lot more than its economic value, and the price rises to two or more times the economic value, driven primarily by rising perceived or psychological value, then we say there is a bubble.

It's important to understand that, in the early stages, every bubble goes up for very logical, economically sound reasons. For example, housing prices may increase because as population grows, more people want houses than there are houses available in a given area. Housing prices may also increase because as incomes rise, more people want to buy more expensive homes, which are in limited supply. In this case, the rising value of real estate is simply a matter of supply and demand. Limited supply and growing demand drive up prices. No matter how expensive homes become, as long as there are underlying economic reasons for the increase in price, there is no real estate bubble.

But sometimes as prices rise for any asset, something else kicks in. Call it wishful thinking or just plain greed. People don't want to miss out on the benefits of owning something that is increasing in value, so more and more people want to buy. As demand goes up so does the price, but in this case, the underlying logical economic parameters are simply not there to support the price rise. After a while, the item in question may be selling for far above its logical economic price, based on logical economic parameters. Instead, the price rise becomes increasingly speculative and is based almost entirely on investment psychology. (For more information about what makes a bubble, please visit our web site at **www.americasbubbleeconomy.com/bubbles.**)

While it's true that perceived value is the only value that matters when buying or selling in any marketplace, it is also true that, sooner or later, you cannot fool all of the people all of the time. Eventually, bubbles burst and perceived values fall to their true economic values. Real, rock-solid economic value rests firmly on real economic parameters, such as real profits, real productivity growth, real wage increases, and real assets gains. Pumped up, over-inflated bubbles do not.

History is littered with countless examples of this, including the recent rise and fall of the Internet Bubble.

Never mind that most Internet companies were operating in the red. Never mind that they often had little or no profits, and virtually no financial foundations from which to build. Never mind that any junior CPA fresh out of college could have easily figured out that the numbers just didn't add up. *This was the mighty Internet!* This was the new economic powerhouse that was going to drive us into the new millennium! The perceived value of high-tech stocks rose almost daily, despite the fact that with very few exceptions, most Internet companies had yet to make a dime, and more importantly, had very limited revenue potential.

Then in March 2000, economic gravity kicked in and the value of Internet-related stocks crashed back down to earth. Billions and billions of investment dollars were lost. Many, many intelligent people were in shock for months, even years. In hindsight, of course, it all seems so obvious now. How could we have been so blind!?

Why Are Bubbles So Hard to See?

Bubbles are hard to see *before* they burst. Why? Because the short-term benefits of believing in them (namely, increasing asset values) are far more seductive than any vague ideas about some future, long-term downside. On the way up, bubbles are all gain and no downside, as long as you get out early enough. On the way up, the good times roll like there's no tomorrow. On the way up, we keep believing in the bubble because we want to believe, and most of the time that's all it takes to keep the bubble party going and growing—at least for a while.

On the flipside, on the way down, previously invisible bubbles become instantly recognizable *after* they burst.

Like waking up with a hangover you didn't anticipate the night before, a bursting bubble can be quite painful as assets that once seemed so solid and promising dissipate like fantasies in the cold light of day.

The only way to enjoy the benefits of a bubble as it goes up, without experiencing pain as it goes down, is to get in early—and more importantly, *get out early*. We all know that when the price of anything is going up, those who buy first make the biggest profits. Conversely, when prices are going down, those who sell sooner rather than later, not only lose the least, they also can position themselves to make huge profits elsewhere.

The trick, of course, is to see—and get out of—the bubble *before* it bursts.

Can We See a Bubble Before It Bursts?

There is no iron-clad, foolproof method for proving or disproving the existence and timing of a bubble. A lot has been written on the subject and we won't bore you with dozens of esoteric studies. When deciding if there is or is not a bubble, reasonable people needn't give themselves a degree in economics to be aware of these two key factors that make bubbles hard to see: 1) Esoteric economists are often too busy dissecting the trees to notice that the forest is on fire; and 2) Any analysis by the financial community, both public and private, rarely amounts to more than a sales pitch. People who have financial interests in making sure you continue to believe in the value of their assets, are often not the most reliable sources of accurate analysis. No used car salesman thinks the price of his vehicles are too high, and even if he did, he probably wouldn't tell you.

Rather than trying to refute every esoteric economic argument or debate every financial cheerleader, we are going to simply lay out for you some very basic, very telling facts, and let reasonable people come to their own common sense conclusions about real or inflated values—one bubble at a time.

If nothing else, the following bubble-by-bubble review should give you pause to reconsider some of the current conventional wisdom. As we've said, you needn't agree with all we say to position yourself now to take advantage of what many will miss. The vast majority of people refuse to see a bubble *before* it bursts—and herein lies a bonanza of opportunities for the lucky few who do.

Our Asset Bubbles Will Fall in Two Stages: First Stage Due to Bubbles Bursting, Second Stage Due to Bad Economy

It is important to point out that all asset bubbles (such as the Stock Market Bubble and the Dollar Bubble) will burst in two stages. The first stage will be the bursting of the recent over-valued price bubble. The second stage will be the additional fall in value due to the significant coming downturn in the economy.

For example, if the value of a house has risen from $200,000 to $300,000 in the last 5 years, the first stage of the bubble fall may be a decline of the recent bubble price back to $200,000. Unfortunately, it doesn't end there. The second stage of the fall will involve a further value decline, below $200,000 (when adjusted for inflation), due to very high interest rates and a very slow economy. With many

U.S. assets and asset bubbles, that second stage decline could be quite significant as well.

Do We Have a Bubble in the Stock Market?

There may be as many ways to analyze today's stock market as there are Blackberries on Wall Street. You can spend days studying the charts and numbers up one side and down the other, but all you really need to know is this:

> *The value of U.S. stocks (blue chip stocks, not hyped high-tech) grew nearly 10 fold in the two decades from 1982 to 2000, while real earnings (adjusted for inflation) increased only three fold over this same time period.*

By contrast, in the previous 54 years from 1928 to 1982, the stock market, as measured by the Dow Jones Industrial Average, grew a much more reasonable three fold during a time of huge economic growth.

If the real, underlying economic value of stocks had actually increased 10 fold in 20 years, we would also have seen a similar rise in real earnings and to some extent, *gross domestic product* (GDP). That didn't happen. Instead, investors have spent two decades making stock values defy gravity in a flurry of excitement that bestselling author Robert Shiller beautifully described in his book *Irrational Exuberance.* As we said before, perceived value is all it takes to set the price in any marketplace. But not forever. At some point, economic gravity kicks in, investors pull out, and the bubble pops.

If a 10-fold increase in 20 years is not enough evidence for you, another way to decide for yourself if there is or is not a bubble in the stock market is to look at an old standby for assessing stock value—the *price-to-earnings* (PE) *ratio*. Under normal conditions, the value of a company's stock is directly related to that company's profits or earnings. When earnings go up, stock values go up. When earnings go down, stock values go down. But what if stock prices (adjusted for inflation) start going up faster than earnings? What if stocks keep on going up and up, no matter what the company's profits? Wouldn't that, by definition, be a bubble?

As of mid 2006, PE Ratios are at about 25, rather than the average of 14–15, clearly indicating that most stocks are currently overvalued. High PE Ratios are fine, as long as everyone keeps playing the game and keeps on buying overvalued stocks. But if anything should happen to spook skittish investors into dumping their overpriced stocks, economic gravity will kick in, a sell-off will ensue, and stock values will drop.

What could possibly spook investors? To answer that we need to see if there are any other bubbles floating around in today's economy.

Do We Have a Bubble in the Value of the Dollar?

As with assessing the stock market, there are dozens of ways to measure the merit of the dollar. Is it overvalued, undervalued, or right where it should be, based on real, underlying economic strength? Rather than give yourself a headache trying to analyze the many different views on this complex subject, here's all you really need to know:

In the last couple of years, the Japanese Central Bank has bought almost a trillion dollars of U.S. currency. The Chinese Central Bank is not far behind, buying a whopping $800 billion of our cash.

Why would a foreign government buy so much of our money? Good question. They do it for one simple reason: to keep the value of our dollar high so we can continue buying lots of their exports.

Here's an even better question: Where would we be right now if China and Japan had *not* bought up almost $2 trillion of our cash? What would the dollar's value be if they hadn't stepped in and propped it up? And more importantly, what will happen to our dollar when they *stop* propping it up?

Exactly when China and Japan will quit buying massive amounts of our dollars is hard to say (as of this writing, Japan has stopped at least temporarily, and is letting China pick up the entire burden), but this much you can count on: Anytime a nation's currency (or any asset, for that matter) has to be bought up in huge numbers in order to maintain its value, that is prima facie evidence of a bubble. Don't be snowed by complicated arguments. You can hold your own in any debate about the true value of any asset simply armed with this one deadly fact: If you have to manipulate it to keep it afloat, it's a bubble. It's that simple.

The more complex question is when will this manipulation stop and the bubble burst—a question we take a stab at answering in Chapter 3. For now, all you need to know is that a solid, economically grounded dollar does not need foreign governments to buy massive amounts of it in order to prop up its value. If it's manipulated, if it's made to levitate despite economic gravity, if it floats like a bubble and it looks like a bubble . . . it's a bubble.

**What's Unusual About America's Bubble Economy?
It's the First Foreign Government-Supported Bubble.**

Throughout history, most financial bubbles have resulted from the actions of private investors. Private investors buy, buy, buy (the bubble goes up), and then they sell, sell, sell (the bubble comes down).

In this case, we have multiple bubbles, one that is government-built and another that is government-supported. Our big Government Deficit Bubble was created over many years when our government kept borrowing more and more money, much of it from foreign investors. But few people realize our overvalued Dollar Bubble is also being supported by government—not our government, but the governments of China, Japan, and other foreign countries that are actively buying dollars to prop up the price.

This is a truly unusual situation. It is like having another nation, let's say Japan, actively buying up our Internet stocks to keep prices high. Of course, they are not buying our dollars to play a speculative game, but to maintain their exports (and jobs) so they can maintain political support back home. But the fact that major national governments are now directly involved in maintaining the value of our currency makes our overvalued Dollar Bubble much larger than it otherwise would be.

And the bigger the bubble, the harder the fall.

In the meantime, as foreign governments frantically buy up dollars to boost its value, folks back home have been buying up real estate like there's no tomorrow.

Do We Have a Bubble in Real Estate?

By the start of 2006, many people believed we had a bubble in real estate values, at least in some areas of the country. It's interesting to note that people seem to be more willing to accept the idea of a bubble in real estate than any other asset bubble, a good sign that the real estate bubble has started to pop. (Remember, bubbles are easier to see *after* they burst).

Other people strongly disagree. They say today's high real estate values are not a bubble but reflect the basic nature of real estate—a limited commodity in high demand that throughout our history has proven to be a good long-term investment. Today's real estate values are high because demand is high. And even if demand levels off, home values will continue to appreciate, only at a slower rate.

So which is it? Real estate bubble or no real estate bubble?

Let's be reasonable and review the facts. In the 20th century, U.S. home prices consistently rose about 1 percent a year (when adjusted for inflation) in response to rising incomes and growing population. More recently, however, home prices have shot up 10, 15, even 25 percent annually, at a time when real wage growth has been essentially flat and population growth is dramatically slowing.

As with the dollar and the stock market, there's no

need to get derailed by complex arguments. Here's the bottom line:

In the last five years, the real estate market has shot up 80 percent, while incomes rose only 2 percent in this same time period (see Figure 1.1).

If the most fundamental drivers of real estate prices—increasing income and growing population—are simply not present, there is no real, rock-solid economic basis for real estate prices, especially on the east and west coasts, to rise 15 to 20 times faster than they had before.

When real wages doubled from 1950 to 1970, it made perfect sense for home prices to rise, too. Today, that economic logic is simply not there. Still, Americans have been borrowing like mad and buying pricier and pricier homes. As we said earlier, perceived value is all that is necessary to set the price of any marketplace. But perceived

Figure 1.1 Income Growth vs. Housing Prices Growth

INCOME UP 2%   HOUSING PRICES UP 80%

Contrary to what many experts say, the rapid growth of housing prices has not been driven by rising income. In fact, it has far exceeded income growth for the last five years.

value cannot levitate forever if the underlying, real economic foundation is missing.

Making matters even more risky, many of our overpriced homes are mortgaged to the hilt, with additional home equity loans and interest-only second mortgages that could become serious liabilities down the road for already overextended consumers. Adjustable-rate loans and interest-only loans have also helped drive up home prices by allowing more people to take advantage of low interest rates to buy more expensive homes than they otherwise could afford.

Even if we had enormous growth in income or population to support this big growth in real estate prices, if mortgage rates go up significantly—and we will show you

"We sold our two-bedroom in the village at a great price and bought the Virgin Islands."

later that they will—then real estate prices will have to go down. Why? Because most of what you buy when you buy a home is money, not real estate. If the price of the money goes up a lot, it will force the price of the real estate to come down or people will not be able to buy. Mortgage rates could rise significantly if the dollar continues to decline. That's because much of the money funding our mortgages now comes from foreign, especially Asian, investors buying mortgage-backed securities. If the dollar is falling, they will demand a higher return for their mortgage investments or just pull out of the mortgage market entirely. If the Federal Reserve raises interest rates in an effort to hold up the value of the dollar, that will force up mortgage rates as well. An increase in mortgage rates will affect all parts of the country, not just the especially frothy east and west coasts. Even markets that are relatively low priced, such as Texas or North Carolina, will be hurt dramatically by a large increase in mortgage rates.

All this adds up to a Real Estate Bubble on the brink of a fall.

**Home Prices Up 80 Percent, Income Up 2 Percent—
Does That Work?**

Many economists and financial analysts say we should not worry about a significant real estate bubble because the rapid growth in home prices over the last five years has been driven by "good fundamentals" such as solid income and job growth.

Sounds good!

Since 2001, real estate prices, nationwide, have jumped 80 percent. That's a whole lot of jumping! We must have one frisky economy to push home values up so high. Let's see how frisky . . .

Oops. Actual income growth has not been so hot. In fact, in the last five years, incomes are only up about 2 percent—that's some of the weakest income growth we've seen in 25 years.

What about jobs? Surely, we must have created a whole lot more jobs to have such a rise in residential real estate values.

However, job growth was flat from 2001 to 2003, and since that time it has only been half of what it was in the late 1990s.

Does anybody really buy the "good fundamentals" argument? Or are we just believing in the Tooth Fairy because there might be a little gift under our pillows in the morning? Of course, we want to believe. Who wouldn't want their home to be worth more tomorrow than it did yesterday?

Some people's view of reality is not how it is, but how they think it should be.

Do We Have a Bubble in Consumer Debt?

A half century ago, we didn't have credit cards. Now we're drowning in them. Collectively, American consumers went from owing a mere $19 billion in loans (excluding home mortgages) in 1950, to a staggering $1.7 trillion of debt in 2005 (see Figure 1.2). Today, we carry all sorts of credit cards, which we use to buy everything from groceries and gas to the latest movies and electronic gizmos. Many Americans make only the minimum payments each billing

Figure 1.2 Growth of Consumer Debt

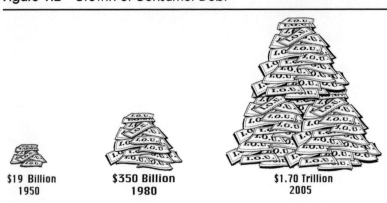

| $19 Billion | $350 Billion | $1.70 Trillion |
| 1950 | 1980 | 2005 |

A key driver of economic growth has been consumer spending and a key driver of consumer spending has been the enormous rise of consumer debt. Will we ever have to pay it back? What will happen to consumer spending and the economy as interest rates rise?

cycle, sometimes using cash advances from one card to cover the smallest required monthly payment of another.

An important reason why credit card spending is at an all time high in America is because it's cheap and easy. Interest rates are exceedingly low because there is so much foreign capital in the United States (foreign investors buy lots of U.S. bonds and many other U.S. assets). As we will see later, if this foreign capital should begin to pull out of the United States (and there are lots of reasons to think it eventually will), our interest rates will go up—way up—and U.S. credit card consumers will be in big trouble.

If we weren't already buying so much on credit, it wouldn't be as big a deal. But buying on credit has become a way of life, almost an addiction, in America. Generations ago, it was common to squirrel away money for a special future purchase. Today, with businesses pushing all kinds of items at low or no interest, and unsolicited credit card offers coming daily in the mail, instant gratification has become the norm.

So is it reasonable to say America faces a bubble in consumer debt?

Look at it this way: If we all quit our credit card habits cold turkey today and continued to make our minimum payments, it would take us many decades to pay it all off. Given that there isn't a chance in the world of that happening, it seems reasonable to say yes, we've got ourselves one heck of a bubble in consumer debt.

The problem with all this credit card debt, aside from the personal financial risk it entails if you lose your job or get sick, is that it makes consumer spending, which now drives over 75% of our economy, extremely vulnerable to a large increase in interest rates. The economy is always sensitive to interest rate increases, especially the Capital Goods Sector (see Chapter 7). The Consumer Debt Bubble increases that vulnerability enormously.

But boy, has buying on credit been a great short term boost to the economy! Right now, all we see are the benefits and they are substantial. Consumer debt is part of the reason our economy has done as well as it has in recent years. Without the credit card boom, we would suffer. The dark side of the Consumer Debt Bubble only appears if interest rates go up a lot. In Chapters 2 and 3, we will show you why we believe interest rates will go higher, much higher—high enough to slow consumer spending on credit and reverse some of the benefits the United States and other economies have enjoyed while the Consumer Debt Bubble was rising.

Do We Have a Bubble in Our International Trade Deficit?

A good deal of what consumers have been buying comes from other countries. The imbalance between what we buy from other nations and what we sell to other countries is called the International Trade Deficit and it is bigger than ever. The trade deficit (the difference between our imports and our exports) means, as we buy more and more goods in today's global marketplace, more and more of our dollars end up in the hands of foreigners. What do foreigners do with all those dollars? They use them to buy our stocks, bonds, real estate, and other assets.

Currently, we import so much more than we export that our astronomical trade deficit has soared to record highs each year and our cumulative trade deficit is now truly massive (see Figures 1.3 and 1.4).

It's important to note that we could not have such a big international trade deficit if we were still on the gold standard, which we went off in 1973 for all international transactions. While we were on the gold standard, we had to keep a certain percentage of gold in reserve to "back" every dollar that flowed out in the world, beyond the United States. We couldn't possibly run a big international trade deficit for very long because if we did we would simply run out of gold. By going off the gold standard for our international transactions, we made it possible for international trade to explode. We also made it possible for our international trade deficit to explode, as well.

We certainly do not advocate going back to the gold standard, but it is important to understand that going off of gold is a relatively new occurence, which helps

Figure 1.3   Growth of the Annual Trade Deficit

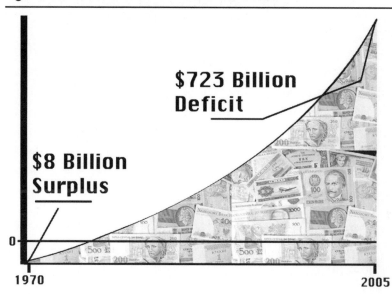

Astronomical growth of the Annual Trade Deficit in the last 10 years puts continuous downward pressure on the dollar. If it were not for large purchases of the dollar by the Japanese and Chinese central banks to prop up its value, the dollar would have fallen long ago.

explain why we have never been in this situation before. (See Chapter 8 for more about how the monetary system has evolved to create America's Bubble Economy, including our current massive International Trade Deficit Bubble.)

Now that we have a huge trade deficit, can we just go on importing foreign goods and export our stocks and bonds forever? Maybe for a while, but only as long as we can maintain a constant value dollar. Like all investors, foreign investors want constant value dollars. They don't want to sell their goods to us for dollars and then have those dollars (their profits) decline in value over time.

Figure 1.4   Growth of the Cumulative Trade Deficit

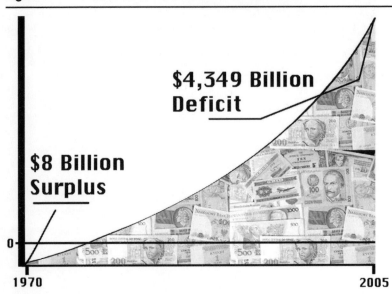

$4,349 Billion Deficit

$8 Billion Surplus

0

1970

2005

The Cumulative Trade Deficit is even more important than the annual number because it provides a rough estimate of how many dollars foreigners are now holding and could begin selling off at any time, especially if the value of the dollar starts to fall.

If the value of our dollar slips, the cost of goods from other nations will automatically rise, in dollar terms. Therefore we won't buy as much of them, which will not be good for their export dependent economies. So anything that pulls our dollar down will not only hurt us at home, it will create an economic downturn around the globe.

But it doesn't stop there. If our dollar declines enough to make foreign investors nervous enough, they will naturally want to sell their U.S. assets and invest elsewhere. This will drive down the value of our assets across the board.

Of course, none of that will happen if we can just

maintain those constant value dollars. We need China and Japan to keep buying our currency in huge numbers to keep our dollar bubble inflated. Reasonable people might say, "No problem!" Those foreign countries will continue to keep us afloat for their own good.

No doubt they will. But for how long? How much money do they have to buy dollars?

A Note on the Trade Deficit

Economists will say that the more accurate way to measure our international trade deficit is to look at the *current account deficit*, which tracks the overall balance of dollars flowing between the United States and other nations. We are purposely avoiding these finer points for the sake of simplicity (and to keep you from falling asleep). A trade deficit is easier for people to understand. It's hard to visualize a "current account" deficit, and in any case, the current account deficit is usually similar in magnitude to the trade deficit, just a bit larger, which only strengthens our basic point: the trade deficit is way too big.

If you'd like more details on the trade or current account deficit, John Williamson, at the Institute for International Economics (IIE), has done some excellent work. You can find him on the IIE web site at **www.iie.com.** The IIE is also an excellent source for information about world trade and economics.

Do We Have a Bubble in U.S. Government Debt?

In 1980, we had a government deficit of only about $50 billion. In 1982, the government decided to triple the deficit to $150 billion. This reasonable amount of deficit spending significantly helped stimulate the economy without many ill effects.

Unfortunately, like a family living the good life on credit cards, deficit spending became so seductive that each year the government borrowed more and more, heavily from foreign investors, until our total government debt (the sum of all our deficit spending, over many years) went from less than $1 trillion in 1980 to an astronomical *$8 trillion* by 2005 (see Figure 1.5).

Figure 1.5   Growth of the Federal Government Deficit

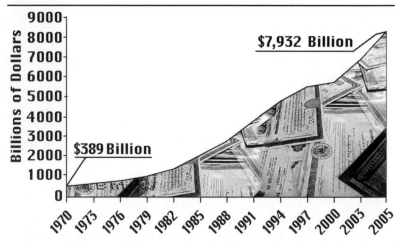

Increasing deficit spending has been a key driver of economic growth and asset value growth for the last two decades. If we had to pay it back, the U.S. economy and U.S. asset values would go massively in reverse. We prefer not to think about that. Instead, we assume we will never have to pay it back and we will be able to refinance at low interest rates forever. Like a family living on credit cards, we have found the miracle cure for all our economic ills.

Your Social Security Taxes Help Fund the Federal Budget Deficit

Few people realize that the government's annual budget deficit is actually much higher than the reported amounts of $350 billion in 2004 and $400 billion in 2005. The actual amount of the deficit was $606 billion in 2004 and $671 billion in 2005.

Why? Because they borrowed the "extra money" from your Social Security Trust Fund, thus reducing the amount of deficit that the government normally reports. Needless to say, the government's accounting practices would never pass muster under the accounting rules that all SEC-reporting corporations must abide by.

From an economic standpoint, though, the "true" deficit is what the government says. That's because tax revenues are covering the deficit, even if those tax revenues are supposed to go to Social Security. As any economist knows, the government can always renege on its Social Security promises. Of course, this might make Social Security recipients a little bit upset.

However, Social Security taxes won't stop. So, when the bubble pops, expect Social Security to survive. But don't expect to get a check unless you really, really need it, because by then they will have to make it means-tested, like a welfare program. If you need the money, some money will be there for you. If you don't, it won't.

Maybe the government should abide by the same accounting rules that it requires of corporations under SEC laws? These laws were designed to give investors an honest picture of a corporation's finances. Maybe the same honesty should be extended to U.S. citizens so they could see where their money is going?

Just a thought.

All this megaborrowing and living beyond our means worked like Miracle Gro on the U.S. economy—interest rates and inflation stayed low, businesses grew, the stock market soared, real estate went through the roof, and the value of the dollar steadily rose.

But like an overextended family with a life style that continually exceeds its income, living large on borrowed capital cannot go on indefinitely. Sooner or later, our $8 trillion IOU is going to turn out to be one heck of a huge liability when foreign investors no longer wish to keep financing our debt-based prosperity.

What could possibly make foreign investors stop lending us money?

Remember the Dollar Bubble? As soon as the value of our already declining dollar begins to significantly fall—and it's only a matter of time before it does—foreign investors are no longer going to find U.S. dollars, U.S. bonds, and other U.S. assets as appealing as they were when the Dollar Bubble was on its way up.

Bubblequake: A Shockwave of Simultaneous Bubble Trouble Around the World

The bursting of any one of the above financial bubbles would create real trouble for the United States and many other nations. Not only are these financial bubbles linked and bound to fall together here in the United States, they also tie the U.S. economy to so many other economies around the world. The bursting of these linked, interdependent bubbles will be nothing the world has experienced before.

Never in our history have all these factors and conditions coexisted at the same time, so it is understandable that many people don't fully appreciate the real dangers we now face. No one can predict the exact moment when our linked bubbles will begin to burst, but this much we know: it's not a matter of *if*, but a matter of *when*.

Based on the common-sense evidence, we have an overvalued Dollar Bubble, an overhyped Stock Market Bubble, a crushing Consumer Debt Bubble, a huge Government Debt Bubble, and an astronomically large International Trade Deficit Bubble. We also have an economy whose continued prosperity depends on unusually low interest rates and low inflation rates, which won't last forever—and a pumped up Real Estate Bubble that is already starting to fall in some areas.

On top of all these dangerous bubbles, there is one other issue that cannot be ignored. Foreign investors now own more U.S. assets than ever before in our nation's history—a massive $12 trillion, all together (see Figure 1.6).

Why does this matter? It matters for a number of reasons we address later, but the most urgent reason is this: Anything that spooks investors to start selling off their U.S. stocks, bonds, dollars, and other assets would have a very negative impact on the value of these assets. In other words, our bubbles will burst and our economy will fall.

Think Internet Bubble . . . times 10.

> ### Can the U.S. Economy Handle a Big Decline in the Dollar? Absolutely!—If That Was Our Only Bubble
>
> Federal Reserve Chairman Ben Bernanke assured us in March 2006 that the economy could withstand a decline in the dollar, even a big decline in the dollar. And he would be absolutely right except for one important fact: Our overvalued dollar is just one of many financial bubbles currently holding up the U.S. economy, including the Stock Market Bubble, the Dollar Bubble, the Consumer Debt Bubble, the International Trade Deficit Bubble, and the astronomical $8 trillion Government Debt Bubble, heavily financed by foreign capital.
>
> If any one of these bubble comes under intense enough pressure, it will put increasing pressure on the others to eventually collide and burst. Popping any one bubble—even our Dollar Bubble—would not create that big a problem. But a chain reaction that ends up popping all the bubbles will be devastating to the U.S. economy.
>
> In Japan, when the stock market (as measured by the Nikkei Average) went from nearly 40,000 to 10,000, it was a big problem, but not devastating. However, if the U.S. stock market (as measured by the Dow Jones Industrial Average) goes from 11,000 to 2,500, it will kick off a chain reaction Bubblequake felt around the world.
>
> So when Chairman Bernanke says the equivalent of "Don't worry, be happy," what he should mean is "Please don't worry enough to kick this thing off."

When America's Bubble Economy pops, almost all the economies of the world will be impacted, most of them harder than the United States. The fact is that the money coming in to finance our bubbles is coming in from

Figure 1.6   Growth of Foreign-held U.S. Assets

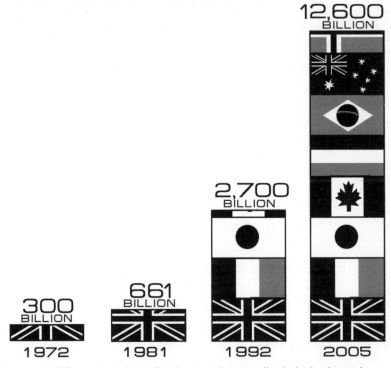

The more U.S. assets held by foreign investors, particularly stocks and bonds, which are very liquid, the more vulnerable our stock market, government, and economy become to a significant decline in the dollar because foreign investors could and would respond by selling off their U.S. assets, driving down their values.

foreign investors. Hence, these investors stand to lose much of that money when the bubbles pop.

In addition, the economies of Europe, the Middle East, and especially Asia are very much tied to their exports to the United States. For decades, the U.S. economy has been the engine of growth for the world. When the dollar significantly declines and the Bubblequake hits, exports to the

31

United States will be devastated. Europe, the Middle East, and Asia will all be hit very hard by the double whammy of huge losses in the value of their U.S. assets and huge declines in their exports. These two conditions will force the local economies into deep recessions.

On the flip side of this gloomy scenario, the sun will be shining brightly. Many of the same opportunities that U.S. investors will have to profit from the popping of the bubbles, will be available to Asian, European, and Middle Eastern investors, as well. Foreign investors will equally benefit from much of the advice we offer U.S. investors in Chapter 5, which also contains separate sections of specific advice for Europeans, Asians, and Middle Easterners.

All the talk about a global economy is true. The economies of the world are increasingly dependent on one another. That means we GROW together and it also means we go SLOW together. When the Bubblequake hits, every nation in the world is in for a very big slowdown. (For more information about the impact of the coming Bubblequake on individuals, businesses, and nations, please visit **www .americasbubbleeconomy.com/howbadcanitget.**)

It Really *Can* Happen Here
(For more details, see Chapters 2 through 4)

Okay, so right about now you are probably thinking that we must be exaggerating a tad. And, honestly, we wish we were. Conventional wisdom certainly would say we are way off the mark, and most people would probably agree.

When talking to people about our ideas for this book, we've found two basic, very understandable (but irrational) responses. The first reaction is: "It can't happen here." The United States of America is the strongest, most successful, and most powerful economy the world has ever known. We call this the "King of the World" defense. The United States has earned the right to be forever successful no matter how badly we manage our financial affairs or how blindly we ignore our problems.

The other, completely opposite, but strangely parallel response is "We're Doomed." So we might as well pretend as if all is well and just keep going, business as usual. If the powerful United States of America is about to face a significant economic downturn, the whole world is hopeless, so we might as well ignore the whole thing and keep going until we run off the edge of the cliff.

A cool-headed, reasonable assessment of the facts shows that both the "King of the World" and the "We're Doomed" crowds are dead wrong; and both groups may well be on their way to being dead broke.

Instead, both groups need to get real. Yes, it really *can* happen here, and yes, you really *can* save yourself and even create tremendous wealth when the bubbles pop by positioning yourself now to be among the smart, realistic few who will benefit from the coming Bubblequake.

Skeptical or not, you already have the book in your hands. At this point, you might as well stick around and find out what we're talking about.

How to Make Huge Profits When the Bubbles Pop
(For more details, see Chapters 5 through 7)

Savvy investors, business owners, and jobseekers needn't roll over or go under when the bubbles burst. Facing facts now, preparing early, and knowing the timing of unfolding events leading up to the coming Bubblequake are your essential keys to discovering how to cover your assets and potentially make huge profits.

Remember, most people will hang onto their "King of the World" or "We're Doomed" positions until the window has closed for doing something smart. Depending on your particular level of wealth and personal level of risk tolerance, we have detailed information we think you will find both insightful and practical.

Don't wait until its too late. Like in any coming disruption, *now* is the time to learn the basics, prepare for the worst, and plan to make the most of this once-in-a-lifetime opportunity to create wealth.

Customized Analysis for Your Specific Industry, Business, or Investment Goals

The authors and their economic experts and experienced business valuators can apply rigorous economic analysis to a variety of industries and businesses, based on the ideas introduced in this book. Individual investors, investment bankers and other investment professionals can also benefit from personalized consulting to suit their particular needs. Country-specific analysis can be customized for rapidly changing conditions in the United States, Europe, Asia, or the Middle East.

For more information, please contact The Foresight Group at 800–994–0018.

The Really Big "Big Picture": Our Current Bubble Economy Is Part of The Broader Evolution of Money and Society
(For more details, see Chapter 8)

For Big Picture thinkers, we have something that we hope you find truly adventurous—or refreshing at a time when "long-term thinking" usually refers to about six months into the past or future. After studying how the economy, technology, and society have transformed since humans first walked the earth, coauthor evolutionary economist David Wiedemer has come to a radical conclusion: The world is not merely changing randomly but is, in fact, slowly and systematically evolving.

Based on Dave's carefully constructed theory, our current bubble troubles are actually part of a messy transition in the much broader evolution of money, beginning with simple barter and evolving to today's global economy.

And if that isn't a big enough Big Picture for you, try this one on for size: This evolution of money is actually part of an even broader evolution of human society, which we call STEP Evolution—the linked, coevolution of Science, Technology, Economic, and Politics. STEP Evolution won't help you figure out where to place your next investment bet; but we think it will give you some fascinating and unusual insights into today's rapidly changing world.

You can let us know what you think about STEP Evolution and the rest of the book at **www.americasbubble economy.com/comments**. Also on our web site, you will find more details than we could fit in the book, as well as the latest updates about the coming financial Bubblequake.

Please note that the references and attribution for most of the statistics, data, and graphs used in this book can be found on our website at **www.americasbubbleeconomy.com/attribution.**

Chapter TWO

Bubble Blind

How We Got Ourselves into This Mess

I f we really do have an economy on the brink of a Bubblequake, if we really do have an overvalued Dollar Bubble, an overhyped Stock Market Bubble, an over-priced Real Estate Bubble, a crushing Consumer Debt Bubble, a giant Trade Deficit Bubble, and an astronomical Government Debt Bubble—all threatening to simultane-ously burst and temporarily rock the U.S. and world economies—wouldn't most people have noticed it by now?

As stunning as it may seem, the answer is no.

It's true that a growing number of people are begin-ning to notice some cracks in our surface prosperity. Some are even starting to reposition their assets in anticipation of the coming changes ahead. But by far the majority of folks are simply going along as if all is well. Even if they realize we have a Real Estate Bubble in some areas of the country, and even if they are also aware that the federal government is now up to its eagle's eyeballs in debt, most people have no idea that coming soon is a rare set of eco-nomic circumstances that has never occurred before now and will probably never occur again. When our bubbles burst, and there is really no way we can avoid it at this point, they will burst relatively quickly, as a group. The unfortunate truth is the simultaneous bursting of several linked financial bubbles will catch many, many otherwise intelligent people totally by surprise.

As former Federal Reserve chairman Alan Greenspan has said in his classic minimizing style: Bubbles can be difficult to recognize *before* they burst. No doubt, the academics could give us lots of complex explanations why this is the case, but the single, most important reason that bubbles are so hard to detect *before* they pop is really quite simple. *We don't want to see them.*

And who could blame us? After all, no one wants to see their wealth, large or small, rapidly shrink or even vanish completely like so much hot air from a popped balloon. It's human nature to want to avoid thinking too much about potential risks. We all want to believe that our assets are as solid as Fort Knox and will continue to grow far into the future. What could be more reasonable?

Or more wrong, as history has repeatedly shown us.

Centuries of Bubble Blindness

Throughout the ages, bubbles have always been largely invisible. No one, for example, could see the Dutch Tulip Bubble before it popped in 1637. Virtually no one saw through the South Seas Stock Bubble until it burst in 1720. No one concerned themselves about the great Florida Land Boom until it went bust in the 1920s. Few investors worried about the intoxicating Stock Market Boom of the roaring 1920s until after it evaporated into the Great Depression in 1929. And only a handful of savvy commentators recognized the irrational exuberance of the Internet Bubble in time to get out before it crashed back to reality in 2000—notably Tony Perkins, who wrote the enormously insightful and prescient book *The Internet Bubble* prior to the Internet stock crash.

It is important to note, as we pointed out in the previous chapter, that in the early stages of every bubble, there are always some good, sound economic justifications for asset values to rise. The trouble is, in a bubble, asset values continue to magically rise and rise and rise. We don't recognize bubbles before they burst because it is human nature to want to believe in miracles, or at least cash in on other people believing in them. In his 1841 classic, *Extraordinary Popular Delusions and the Madness of Crowds,* Charles Mackay says irrational group behavior drives otherwise sane people to run off the edge of cliffs while trying to grab at imaginary gold rings. Bubbles grow, he says, because people are far more motivated to believe in them than to face facts.

All it takes to get a bubble off the ground is for a few people to act as if something is growing in value, even when there is no underlying economic justification to support that growth. In time, additional people—not wanting to miss out—join in, further inflating the bubble. Soon critical mass is reached and nearly everyone wants a piece of the action, further driving up demand and therefore the price. Artificially elevated asset values can continue for quite a while as long as everyone keeps playing the game. But as soon as some bit of reality interrupts the game and triggers a sell-off, people then rush to get rid of the now-not-so-valuable asset. Demand drops, the bubble bursts, and asset values crash back to earth.

By way of example, economists enjoy reminding us of the Dutch Tulip Bubble of 1637, probably because it happened a long time ago and probably because it involved flowers—allowing the rest of us the comfort of thinking of ourselves as too savvy to fall for such foolishness. Focusing on the Dutch tulip craze lets us analyze a bubble while retaining some semblance of dignity. In truth, we are just as gullible and just as greedy as the temporary tulip mongers. Although the culture of that time was quite different from today, the basic psychology certainly is not.

In the early 1600s, many wealthy people in the Netherlands became swept away in a tulip craze, elevating the price of tulip bulbs to dizzying heights, with more and more people trying to get their hands on the valuable flowers and traders paying the equivalent of thousands of dollars for a single bulb. Soon, the plant itself became a secondary issue. As the price shot up, people began buying tulip bulbs for resale and for status. In time, tulip exchanges were established and jobbers manipulated the price. Up from dirt, tulip bulbs had magically become living diamonds.

Of course, being tulip bulbs and not diamonds, it was only a matter of time before some people began to worry that the high price of tulip bulbs might (pardon our pun) return to earth. As soon as enough people became worried enough, the price of tulips wilted like a cut flower. During the height of tulip mania, it was common knowledge that tulips were quite valuable. Once prices crashed back to earth, it was common knowledge that a bubble had popped. Same tulips, same people. Only difference was, before the bubble popped, no one could see a bubble; and after the bubble popped, no one could see why they couldn't see a bubble.

If you think we are so different today, think again. As John Kenneth Galbraith so aptly points out in his 2004 book, *The Economics of Innocent Fraud*, most bubbles exist precisely *because* people refuse see them. Bubbles grow when we take seemingly "innocent" actions designed to purposely ignore the facts so we can capitalize on the moment. Like starry-eyed teenagers on a beer-soaked joyride into the warm summer night, everything seems possible. A few hours later, with the front bumper wrapped around a tree, steam hissing from the radiator, and several painful bumps swelling on their "innocent" heads, the party is over and incredulous adults are left asking: "What in the world were you thinking?!"

The Joyride Begins: How We Created Our Current Bubbles by Running Big Foreign-Funded Government Deficits

It all started out innocently enough with just a few simple actions, really, nothing complicated. But sometimes a few simple actions can lead to some very big, very complex consequences.

The beginning of our current bubble troubles began uneventfully back in 1982 when our government wanted to spend more money than it had in income. This is easy to understand. There are always things that we may want that we don't have the immediate money to buy. So you borrow a little—and nothing necessarily wrong with that.

In 1982, the federal government borrowed $150 billion, about three times the deficit of 1980, just enough to have a wonderfully stimulating effect on the sagging U.S. economy. This deficit spending did what an appropriate amount of deficit spending is supposed to do—it "primed the pump" without choking the engine. The debt was large enough to jump start the economy, but not so large we couldn't pay it off with tax money in a reasonable amount of time. A measly $150 billion is not that much from a national economic standpoint, a molehill, really.

Unfortunately, in 1983, we borrowed a little more. We did so again in 1984, again in 1985, and again and again for almost every year until our little helpful molehill grew into a huge mountain of debt, soaring to more than $8 trillion by 2005. As we will see later, this turned out to be the biggest, stupidest economic mistake the United States has ever made. (For more information, see **www.americasbubbleeconomy.com/feddeficits**.)

Most of us have a hard time comprehending the enormity of $8 trillion dollars. Here's a quick way to visualize it. Imagine that you have just been handed a crisp one dollar bill. Moments later, you are handed another dollar, and then another, and then another. After a while, your bundle of cash becomes too bulky, so you place it on a table, as more and more money is added to the pile. At $8,000, your stack of tightly packed one dollar bills would tower over your head, almost reaching the ceiling. Very impressive.

At *$8 trillion*, your stack of dollars would tower more than 800,000 miles above the Earth—more than three times the distance to the moon. Even in today's global economy, I think we can agree that $8 trillion is one serious IOU.

And it gets worse.

In addition to the sheer astronomical size of our government debt, the other troublesome reality concerns *to whom*, we now owe this mind-boggling tower of debt. If the amount we wanted to borrow had been "smaller"—as

"Our deficit-reduction plan is simple, but it will require a great deal of money."

in mere billions of dollars—the federal government could have simply borrowed it from our fellow citizens. But borrowing a tower of dollars more than three times the distance to the moon from American citizens would never have worked. Such a huge demand for money from U.S. investors would have forced interest rates sky high and slowed the economy to a crawl. That's because interest rates rise and fall, based on supply and demand. High demand for money would have pushed interest rates up, putting the brakes on business and personal spending and significantly slowing the economy. Nobody wanted that.

The other option was simply to print 800,000 miles of money, but that would just drive up inflation, again slowing the economy. Nobody wanted that, either. We could also just save enormously, but nobody wanted to do that either and it would hurt the economy by reducing spending.

The solution to this problem turned out to be quite effective: Borrow it from foreigners. Borrowing from foreigners provided all the money our government wanted to spend on things that we really couldn't afford, while keeping our interest and inflation rates low. To be fair, the government didn't exactly plan it this way; it just sort of happened over time. The government wanted to spend more money without raising taxes, and foreign investors were becoming increasingly wealthy and increasingly eager for places to invest. The credit-worthiness of the United States was sterling, and our U.S. bonds were practically risk-free. So they lent and we borrowed. It would have been a match made in heaven, if it weren't for . . . the catch.

The Catch: We Have to Repay Our Big Foreign-Funded Debt with "Constant Value" Dollars

Here's where things get dangerous. If we borrow a stack of dollars that is three times taller than the moon, we have to repay those debts in what economists call *constant-value dollars*—meaning these dollars must maintain their value, relative to other currencies around the globe. No investor wants to be repaid in dollars that are worth far less than the original dollars they lent. Foreign investors want constant-value dollars, or better yet, rising-value dollars.

Luckily for them—and for our entire economy— rising-value dollars are exactly what they got. With foreign investors lending and investing so much money in the United States, our economy grew like wildfire and the value of the dollar shot up. This made everyone very, very happy.

Foreign investors became very excited, even ecstatic. Not only could they make a profit on our low-risk U.S. Treasury bonds, they could also make an additional profit simply from the rising value of the dollar. Even without the rise in the dollar, the bonds alone would have been a good deal because the odds of the U.S. government not repaying its debts was near zero.

Huge Foreign-Funded Deficits Boom the Economy

Meanwhile, the rest of the country was quite happy, too. Financing huge government deficits with foreign capital greatly stimulated our economy with almost no ill effects. Instead of hurting our nation, big federal deficits were an enormous boost to our economy. Stoked with so much foreign cash, the nation's economy took off like a convertible full of teenagers on Friday night. The tremendous advantages of borrowing large amounts of money from foreigners to fund huge government deficits were irresistible, and the results have been nothing short of miraculous for the U.S. economy since 1982.

For starters, the huge supply on foreign money helped drive down interest rates and inflation, beginning in 1982, which pushed up the value of many U.S. assets. Falling interest rates encouraged the purchase of capital goods, such as cars and houses, and made credit cards cheaper and easier to obtain, creating a growing pool of capital to buy more and more goods. Falling interest rates also helped businesses rapidly expand, offering consumers more and more goods and services to buy with cash or credit. And falling interest rates boosted the value of equity, both public and private, so stock market prices began to rise.

Huge deficit spending, made possible by foreign money, helped build our military and bought us all sorts of goods and services while avoiding tax hikes, further stimulating the economy.

In turn, the booming economy added fuel to the stock market fire as joyful investors began grabbing up stocks at higher and higher prices. For an excellent discussion of stock market bubble, we highly recommend Robert Shiller's groundbreaking book *Irrational Exuberance*. It is simply the best on the subject.

"That's me back in '98, when I was irrationally exuberant."

A booming stock market encouraged even more foreigners and Americans to buy stocks, further driving up the markets. From 1982 when the borrowing started, to 2000, the Dow increased tenfold and the NASDAQ was up over 25 times. Even after the correction of 2000, both the Dow and the NASDAQ are still each up almost 10 times since 1982. Company earning did not increase at the same rate during this period, which explains why PE ratios (comparing stock price to company earnings) rose so dramatically during this period, indicating that stock prices have inflated faster than earnings (see Figure 2.1).

Having a stock market that increased tenfold in 20 years has worked like Miracle-Gro on the U.S. economy.

Figure 2.1   Growth of the P/E Ratio

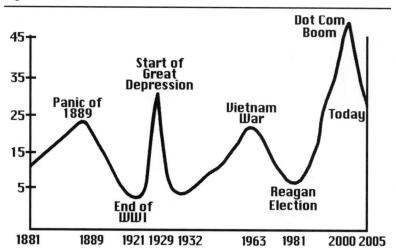

One traditional and still valuable way to see if the stock market is over valued is to look at the Price/Earnings Ratio. Historically, the P/E Ratio has fluctuated around 14, meaning the price of stocks (as measured by the S&P Composite Index) has generally been about 14 times greater than company earnings. Recently, the P/E Ratio has been about 25.

Businesses grew, jobs were created, and consumers kept consuming. Real estate began to appreciate nicely. The growing demand for dollars to buy valuable American real estate, stocks, and bonds, greatly increased the value of the dollar, allowing foreigner investors to make *even more money* on their already spectacular investments. Returns like these on U.S. stocks, bonds, and real estate have hardly ever been seen in the modern industrial world. More and more foreigners came looking to lend and invest more and more money, further driving up the value of our assets, including our currency.

As a wonderful bonus, the high price of the dollar also made foreign goods spectacularly cheap for American consumers, who by now were armed with wallets full of credit cards and low interest home equity loans, often used to pay their credit cards and buy more imported goodies. The explosion in imported foreign goods flowing into the United States was great news for the nations who sold us these goods. Many economies around the world began to grow along with us. Some, like China, grew even faster than the United States. With the value of the dollar high, and less prosperous nations working around the clock to make cheap stuff for us to buy, the world became one big Wal-Mart to American consumers.

The economic advantages of borrowing huge amounts of money from foreigners to fund astronomical government deficits are almost too many to list. To summarize, a quick review of the benefits shows how important big influxes of foreign capital have been—and continue to be—for our economy:

1. The huge supply on foreign money helps keep interest rates low.

2. The government uses this money to fund its deficits. This deficit spending is highly simulative of the economy. It allows for lower taxes and more jobs created by government spending.

3. Low interest rates encourage purchases of capital goods such as cars and houses.

4. Low interest rates help make credit cards cheaper and easier to obtain, creating a growing pool of capital to buy more goods (and a credit card industry boom).

5. Low interest rates allow business to expand more easily.

6. Low interest rates also help the stock market. Without getting into equity valuation theory too much, suffice to say that the lower the interest rates the higher the value of equity, public and private. The value of stocks start to grow rapidly.

7. The booming economy created by the above listed factors add more fuel to the stock market fire.

8. A booming stock market encourages foreigners to put even more capital into the United States by investing in the stock market.

9. The huge surge in the stock market encourages even more foreigners and Americans to invest. The market went up over 10 times from 1982, the start of the borrowing, to 2000. The NASDAQ was up over 25 times!!! What a country! Who wouldn't invest! (The Dow is still up almost 10 times as is the NASDAQ even after the correction of 2000—not bad at all).

10. With the stock market and economy booming, real estate also begins to appreciate.

11. The huge demand for dollars to buy American stocks, bonds and real estate, greatly increases the value of the dollar. Foreigners are making even more money on their already spectacular investments. Investment returns like these on stocks, bonds and real estate have hardly ever been seen in the modern industrial world.

12. The high price of the dollar also makes foreign goods spectacularly cheap to American consumers who are now armed with lots of credit cards and low interest home equity loans (sometimes used to pay off the credit cards) to buy those foreign goods. An explosion in purchases of foreign goods results.

Thank Heaven for Massive Government Deficits

Many people, including former Federal Reserve Chairman Alan Greenspan, have said big government deficits are a threat to our economy. And of course, this it true. However, there's another side to running a government deficit that—for some strange reason—almost no one ever talks about, even though it's easy enough for anyone to see.

The big secret that most experts never, ever discuss is this: Running a big government deficit has an incredibly powerful positive impact on the economy and on most asset values—in the short term.

Economists know that deficit spending can significantly stimulate the economy, and they even have a name for it: "priming the pump." The government borrows money and uses it to buy goods and services. The people

---

receiving this money then spend it on more goods and services, and so on, creating an increase in economic activity. Since there is no offset in the form of taxes (the government is borrowing the money, not taking it from taxes), deficit spending can be a big boost to economic growth.

There are limits, of course. If the government borrows too much money, then the increased demand for money pushes up interest rates (the cost of money).

Now here comes the part that almost no one is willing to talk about, even though they know it. The wonderful solution to this problem is to *borrow the money from foreigners.*

Borrowing from foreigner investors means there is much less, if any, "crowding out" of money for U.S. businesses and individuals. Instead, because U.S. capital is not sucked up by the government, it is available for other uses, keeping interest rates down and stimulating the economy. Massive government deficits, now totaling nearly $8 trillion in government debt, *heavily funded by foreign capital*, have an enormously positive impact on the economy. It's practically a gift from heaven. It's been the Underdog Super Power Pill of economic growth! Stock prices are way up in the last 25 years, real estate values went sky high, and other U.S. assets have done very, very well.

It's perfect!

Well, not quite perfect—and herein lies the reason no one is singing its praises. Eventually, we do have to pay it all back. And then, all that positive will turn to negative when it's time to pay the bill.

And here's the real kicker, and the real reason why no one says a word about the wonderful benefits of running huge government deficits heavily funded by foreigners: We don't have to pay it back to American investors, we have to pay it back to *foreign investors*, which means as soon as they want out, they are going to start selling off their U.S. assets, and all those wonderful asset values are going to crash back down to earth.

Can't we just keep borrowing forever? No, we can't, because at some point we will owe so much no one will want to risk lending to us anymore.

Well, won't that just be our grandchildren's problem, not ours?

We think not, but you can come to your own conclusion when you read Chapter 3. For now, know this: The bigger our bubbles, including the Government Debt Bubble, the more imbalances they create in the economy that are harder to maintain than most people think. With imbalances this big, it won't take that much of a shove to set off a chain reaction of colliding bubbles, ending in collapse.

Will that actually happen? Read the next chapter and tell us what you think at **www.americasbubbleeconomy .com/comments.**

Sounds Wonderful! But Remember the Catch: We Have to Repay with "Constant Value" Dollars

All this debt-based, gravity-defying prosperity comes with one heck of a huge price tag: the painful fall back to earth.

Why would there ever be a fall? Can't it just keep going like this forever? Possibly it could, if it wasn't for that one little catch we mentioned earlier: Foreign investors, like all investors, want to be repaid in constant-value dollars. They want dollars that maintain their value

"You know, sometimes, just to convince myself that the eighties really happened, I go down to the vault and look at my money."

compared to other currencies. Otherwise, they lose their profits as the value of the dollar falls. If that happens, they won't want to keep lending us more money.

To keep the party going, we need more money on a regular basis. Diamonds may last forever, but government bonds do not. We have to continuously pay off old bonds (repay old debt) and sell new bonds (create new debt). As long as we can keep repaying investors in constant-value dollars, investors will want to keep buying our bonds and other assets, and our huge megadebt party will keep going and growing.

When we fail to repay investors with constant-value dollars, and instead they begin to see the value of their dollars fall dramatically, relative to other currencies, the party is going to come to a screeching halt. Foreign investors will no longer want to buy U.S. bonds, dollars, or stocks, and the appeal of many other U.S. assets will also rapidly fade. Instead, investors will want to sell off their various U.S. assets, while prices are still relatively high.

Of course, the U.S. government has to continue to sell bonds, and with fewer buyers wanting to buy our bonds, interest rates will automatically rise. The more the demand for bonds drop, the higher interest rates climb. Just as falling interest rates, beginning in 1982, drove stock and other U.S. assets values up, rising interest rates drive stock and other U.S. asset values down.

As asset values fall, more and more investors (both foreign and American) want to sell before asset prices go too low. "Rational panic" sets in as more and more investors want out. The supply of U.S. dollars, stocks, bonds, and other assets shoot up as more and more people want to sell. Demand drastically drops as less and less people want to buy. High supply and low demand equals low price.

With the value of the dollar dropping, the U.S. government eventually has little choice but to print more dollars—driving up inflation and further decreasing the buying power of the dollar. U.S.-asset values will begin to crash and the bubbles will begin to pop.

Just as foreign investors helped create our booming economy since 1982, foreign investors increasingly hold the fate of our future economy in their hands. As long as we keep feeding them constant-value dollars, all will be well. As soon as we try to give them falling-value dollars, they are going to want to get rid of their overvalued U.S. assets, deflating our bubbles, and allowing America's Bubble Economy to burst.

Why Do Foreign Investors Now Have So Much Influence Over Our Future Economy?

The disturbing answer is: Because we sold it to them.

Foreigners now hold more than $12 trillion in U.S. assets, including our stocks, bonds, real estate, and more. Even if you can't quite buy the idea that the United States is operating in a Bubble Economy, you have to admit that if foreign investors ever decide to unload even 10 to 20 percent of their current U.S. assets, the value of those assets, including the value of the dollar, would drop like a lead balloon. Bubble or no bubble, a falling dollar does not a booming economy make. To stay prosperous and to keep our foreign investors happy, we absolutely must have constant-value (or better yet, rising-value) dollars.

Protecting the Almighty Dollar

What is keeping it from falling right now? Again, our fate lies in the hands of foreigners.

Currently, the value of the dollar is carefully protected by the central banks of various countries, including the United States, China, Japan, and others (see Figure 2.2). Whenever any government buys a currency, it increases the demand for that currency and therefore increases or at least maintains its price, just as increased demand would increase the price of any commodity.

Figure 2.2   U.S. Dollars Held by Other Nations

Japan	$832 billion
China	$818 billion
Taiwan	$255 billion
Korea	$205 billion
Hong Kong	$125 billion

Dollars held by Central Banks of Foreign Nations in 2005

When governments buy dollars, the increased value of the dollar lures private investors back into the dollar markets, further strengthening the dollar.

Japan and China are highly motivated to support our dollar so that we will continue to buy their exports and keep their workers employed. As of 2005, the Japanese and Chinese central banks have bought a massive $1.75 trillion worth of U.S. dollars in order to prop up the value of our currency. When Japan stopped buying dollars at the end of the first quarter of 2004, China stepped in and picked up the slack (see Figure 2.3).

But even with all this support, our precious dollar—upon which our entire economy now depends—is hardly risk-free. In recent years, it has been losing ground compared to the European Union currency, the euro. And the price of gold has been steadily rising, also indicating slipping confidence in the dollar. We will have much more to say about gold later, but for now it's important to understand that, historically, the market value of gold is inversely proportional to investor confidence in the dollar.

Figure 2.3 Japanese and Chinese Central Bank Purchases of Dollars

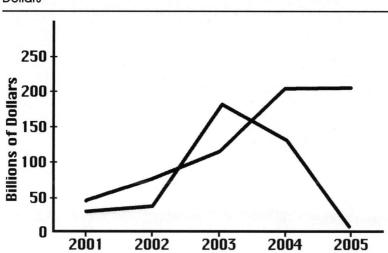

China's and Japan's central banks have both protected the value of our currency by purchasing many, many dollars over the last several years. After the first quarter of 2004, Japan completely stopped buying dollars and China picked up the slack. How long can China handle such a burden with an economy only a third the size of Japan? What will happen when they, too, can no longer buy dollars?

In other words, gold is strong when the dollar is weak. Gold prices almost doubled from January 2001 to January 2006. The value of the dollar fell 20 percent in that same period.

The Dollar Is a Commodity

It's easy to think of money only as a means to trade goods and services. In fact, dollars, themselves, are traded as a commodity in the world marketplace, bought and sold like so many pork bellies. On the Foreign Exchange Market, the price of the dollar and other currencies goes up and down, depending on supply and demand. Rising demand creates rising value; falling demand results in falling value.

Over the last several years, the sheer volume of currencies traded on the Foreign Exchange Market has grown astronomically:

- $5 billion/day in 1970
- $50 billion/day in 1980
- $100 billion/day in 1990
- $1.5 trillion/day in 2000
- $1.9 trillion/day in 2004

As on this writing, a staggering $1.3 billion worth of currencies exchange hands every minute of every business day. That's about $100 million in the time it took you to read this sentence!

What Will Pop the Dollar Bubble?

With such massive international support, what could possibly set the dollar on a downward spiral? The initial cause may be dramatic or insidious; major or minor; happening all at once or in small, painful increments, like being eaten by ants. The most likely possibilities for triggering a significant decline in the dollar include:

- A continued loss of foreign investor interest in the less-than-spectacular U.S. stock market, causing stock prices to flatten or fall.

- An ever-rising trade deficit, requiring more and more dollars, which private investors become less and less interested in supplying.

- A rapid decline in investor confidence due to an unlikely dramatic event, like a major terrorist attack or a devastating medical pandemic, such as bird flu.

- A gradual decline in investor confidence due to a generally faltering U.S. economy.

- A drop in mortgage backed securities due to falling real estate values or rising interest rates. Foreign investors hold a lot of U.S. mortgages.

- Good performance by foreign stocks and other foreign assets, which is already occurring.

- Continued unrest in the Middle East or a disruption of the oil supply.

Whatever the trigger, once the dollar begins to significantly slip, our government, along with our trading partners such as China and Japan, will do all they can to prop up its value. But central banks are not super heroes. They can only do so much before succumbing to the strain of having to buy increasing numbers of dollars. Just like in the United States, remember, the central banks of foreign governments have to use real money to buy our dollars and there are only three ways their governments can get real money—either tax their citizens, print more money and raise inflation, or sell more bonds. Too many taxes and too much inflation eventually pose real problems for any nation.

As much as they will want to support the dollar for the good of their own economies, the time will inevitably come when central banks are going to say enough is enough. Once they step aside, our already sagging Dollar Bubble will have no choice but to seriously fall.

In the meantime, the United States and other governments continue to protect and support the dollar (for more information, see **www.americasbubbleeconomy.com/supportdollar).** No economy in the world wants to see our currency fail; and even those nations that are not now buying dollars may join in the fight to save the dollar in a massive last-ditch effort to avoid the unavoidable. China will likely continue to buy our dollars until they can buy no more. Eventually, they will simply run out of money to buy our currency, and the dollar will fall.

Even for Us, the Idea that America Has a Bubble Economy is Almost Too Hard to Believe

As authors of this book, we're not supposed to say we have a hard time believing our own conclusions. But, in a sense, we do. This is, after all the United States of America, the powerful and prosperous country we grew up in, not some debt-ridden South American dictatorship.

But here's another way to look at it that may help us all face facts: What if another country, not our beloved America, was doing what we are doing? What would we think of that?

What if, instead of the United States, some smaller dictatorship nation went deeply into debt to stimulate its economy, and as a result, its stock and real estate values went sky high? And what if that country used huge amounts of foreign capital to help finance that debt, rather than loans from its own citizens?

And what if the general population of this other

---

country also went deeply into debt without much savings, and this consumer debt was also partly funded by foreigners, further stimulating the economy?

Would you consider all that a good long-term plan for growth? Or a recipe for inevitable disaster?

So what makes the United States so different?

Well, for one thing we have a much larger and much stronger economy than, say, Argentina, so we can borrow much more money. Argentina, on the other hand, would collapse under a relatively small amount of debt, like $100 billion, while we can easily borrow trillions of dollars.

We also have a much better reputation for sound economic management than other countries giving us a very good "credit rating" with both domestic and foreign investors. Unlike other countries, our government has never taken on such a massive amount of debt from foreigners to fund its current expenses. And, our citizens have never taken on such massive amounts of debt to fund our consumption. We've always been good savers—until recently. Now we are the world's best consumers, and world's worst savers.

Given our huge economy and our great credit standing, we can certainly borrow much more money for a much longer period of time than a small debt-ridden country, but are we entirely and forever immune to the problems the smaller debt-ridden country will face?

The answer seems so hard to believe, but obviously it has to be *no*—we are not entirely and forever immune.

We are also closer to the edge than it would seem given that we have no more ability to pay off our $8 trillion government debt than a debt-ridden South American dictatorship has of paying off its $100 billion government debt. It's really not all that different, other than the amount of money involved.

Would a banker be any more likely to lend money to

someone who has massive debts that he can't possibly pay off, than to someone who has a much smaller debt that he can't possibly pay off? Maybe for a while the bank will continue to lend to the richer debtor because he has a better credit rating, but eventually the banker will have to stop lending or he'll lose all his money.

Bubblequake, Our Simultaneous Bubble Trouble: One Pops and They All Fall

The popping of any one bubble will quickly drag the other ones down. It could start with the Real Estate Bubble bursting, followed by the Stock Market Bubble, and then the Dollar Bubble. No matter what sets things in motion, once the Dollar Bubble significantly begins to slide, the rest of our linked financial bubbles are going to simultaneously crash as more and more investors sell their U.S. assets.

With fewer private foreign investors wanting to buy our bonds, interest rates will automatically rise. Rising interest rates drive stock values down. With rising interest rates and a falling dollar, skittish investors will naturally want to unload their overvalued U.S. stocks. As soon as enough people start pulling out, the flood gates open and the stock market falls fast. Remember, stocks are overvalued, based on real earnings, so this "adjustment" brings stocks more in alignment with what they are really worth. Unfortunately, the markets will probably dip even lower, at least for a while.

But our problems won't stop there. With the U.S. stock market significantly declining, that further deflates the value of the dollar. Falling stock markets and a declining dollar will add fuel to the fire around the globe, pushing more and more investors to sell off their dollars and other U.S. assets in a mad dash to limit losses and make spectacular profits by buying gold, euros, and yen. Big shots like Warren Buffet, Bill Gates, and George Soros are already on this track to some extent. After central banks can no longer prop up the dollar, nearly every investor on the planet will want to join them.

Meanwhile, the slowing U.S. economy hurts U.S. businesses in nearly every sector and drives up unemployment across the board. A diminished dollar will make us less able to buy as much as we currently import from other nations, which, in turn, hits many economies very hard, causing unemployment to rise around the globe.

If they haven't already, real estate prices will fall across the country, from New York to San Francisco and beyond. Interest rates and inflation will climb, greatly reducing business growth, consumer spending, and government spending. Exports from other countries will dramatically decline, sending financial tremors around the globe. Unemployment will spike, banks will go under, and whole industries will wilt all across the planet.

Are we exaggerating? We certainly hope so. But all the evidence is there for reasonable people to see, no matter how much we wish it wasn't.

From its peak in 2000 to mid 2006, the stock market is down, way down. The NASDAQ is down 50 percent, the S&P is down 25 percent, and the Dow is down 5 percent. Although the stock market climbed up from its 2002 lows, it remained essentially flat in 2004 and 2005. Certainly, these are not the glory days of the 1980s and 1990s, which lured in so much foreign money.

On the all-important dollar side, the Japanese, who used to buy massive amounts of dollars and still have the largest dollar reserves at nearly $1 trillion, have not bought a single greenback since March 2004. Fortunately, China picked up the slack in 2004, quadrupling their previous dollar purchases. China bought more than $30 billion per month in the last quarter of 2004. More recently, however, they are showing some signs of "dollar fatigue." Even if they wanted to buy more, at some point, they simply won't be able to. Japan has already dropped out of the game, at least since March of 2004. China is having to do double duty to make up for the loss of Japan's buying power but with a much smaller economy than Japan's. At some point, perhaps very soon, China will be forced to drop out of the game as well.

The Europeans are currently able, but so far unwilling to manipulate the value of the dollar in this way. Perhaps as a crisis begins, they will step in. Unfortunately, by then the value of the falling dollar will be much, much harder to control with government intervention.

Profit When It Pops—with Alternative Investments

Never in history have we been on the brink of a more dangerous global bubble collapse. We couldn't have planned it this way if we tried. And of course, we wouldn't want to. But we can plan to protect ourselves, our families, and our businesses from its impact. And we can even plan to profit from it by understanding what will happen, when it will happen, and best of all, how to milk it for all its worth.

Unlike during most economic downturns, the coming Bubblequake will offer smart, reasonable people the rare opportunity to cash in on several alternative investments (discussed in detail Chapters 5–7).

The key to making big profits when the bubbles burst is *timing*. Knowing what's coming before it hits will allow you to recognize what others will initially miss and will help guide your moves. Timing is essential. So before we dive into the details of how to cash in on the coming chaos, let's take a closer look at how the dominoes will likely fall.

Chapter THREE

Bubblequake

A Likely Scenario of How Our Bubbles Will Collide and Fall

Despite the persistent chorus of economic cheer-leading insisting all is well, the price for the biggest, stupidest economic mistake the United States has ever made—borrowing a tower of money from foreign investors more than three times taller than the moon—will inevitably crash down on us. Like a bustling city built precariously on a fault line, most Americans have no idea that a financial earthquake is about to rattle their world in the next few years.

Smart and reasonable people who see it coming can prepare ahead of time to cover their assets and potentially make huge profits on the coming Bubblequake. To join the fortunate few, it is important to understand what will happen and to track the timing of events so that you can come to your own reasonable conclusions and make your own well-thought-out moves. (For details and updates about timing the Bubblequake, visit **www.americasbubbleeconomy .com/timing.**)

What follows is our best guess about how and when

the coming Bubblequake will occur. Before we venture into the realm of rational speculation, let's review what we already know:

- We know our dollar is overvalued because the Chinese and Japanese have bought $1.75 trillion of our dollars to prop up its price. Therefore we have an artificially inflated Dollar Bubble.

- We know our stocks are overpriced because the Dow has increased 10-fold in 20 years, without an equal rise in real earnings. Therefore we have an overvalued Stock Market Bubble.

- We know our homes are overvalued because personal incomes and population growth have not increased at any where near the same pace. Therefore we have an overpriced Real Estate Bubble.

- We know we have too much consumer debt, compared to our incomes and we are very vulnerable if we enter a period of high interest rates. Therefore we have an overextended Consumer Debt Bubble.

- We know we import far more than we export, with the difference nearing $1 trillion annually. Therefore we have a huge International Trade Deficit Bubble.

- We know we have astronomical government debt, now at more than $8 trillion, which is heavily funded by foreign capital that may not wish to stay forever. Therefore we have a vulnerable Government Deficit Bubble.

Certainly, anyone who ran their personal finances this way would be living on the brink of disaster. No breadwinner can support his family indefinitely by borrowing far more money than he earns. No homeowner in her right mind would take out a 30-year mortgage from a banker who could show up at her door at any time of the day or night and demand the entire note be paid in full on a moment's notice. Yet that is exactly the position we have put ourselves in with our astronomical debt to foreign investors, who now hold huge amounts of our stocks, government debt, and private debts—and who may not wish to do so for too much longer.

Any day now, they're gonna come a callin'.

What Will Cause Our Bubbles to Fall? A Change in Long-term Investor Psychology

It would be far more dramatic if we could say that the U.S. Bubble Economy will fall because of some single, extraordinary event, such as a terrorist attack or a worldwide pandemic of bird flu. While such terrible events are always possible, a big dramatic trigger is far less likely than simply a long, slow squeeze. Rather than being shot with a single bullet, our bubbles will most likely deflate due to a slow and insidious change in long-term investor psychology, although a single bad event might hasten that change.

Even if a dramatic negative event does occur, it cannot, in and of itself, do lasting damage to the economy unless long-term investor psychology has significantly changed. A single event could no more trigger an explosion than a detonator can without any dynamite next to it. The explosive has to build up before it can be detonated.

Looking at past bubbles, it's easy to see this pattern. No great event caused the October 1929 stock market crash that led to the Great Depression. No big tragedy pre-cipitated the bursting of the Internet Bubble in March 2000. And no monumental moment of insight led to the universal loss of interest in buying a single 17th century Dutch tulip bulb for twice the value of one's home. In each case, the only thing different about the day the bub-ble popped, compared to the day before it popped, was simply *a* shift in investor psychology.

This makes perfect sense. After all, bubbles go up because of investor psychology, so naturally, a change in investor psychology is all it takes to bring them down. Group psychology is so profoundly linked to inflating, maintaining, and destroying a bubble, that even if a big destabilizing event does happen to occur, such as a war or an epidemic, it alone cannot make a bubble fall—unless that dramatic event also happens to coincide with a shift in long-term investor psychology. As we saw after the ter-rorist attacks of 9/11, big negative events can have a tem-porary negative impact on the economy. But unless long-term psychology has significantly changed, the eco-nomic dip eventually reverses itself and the bubble stays afloat—at least for a while.

What Will Change Long-Term Investor Psychology? A Flat Stock Market Vulnerable to Shocks

As with every issues we discuss in this book, the experts can and do spend years analyzing all the data and debating every detail. You can drive yourself crazy trying to track every argument, or you can bypass the trees and step back to see the forest. The most likely cause of a change in long-term investor psychology is not likely to be the usual suspects, such as terrorism, rising oil prices, or the out-sourcing of U.S. jobs. Far more likely, investor psychology will turn increasingly negative simply because of the flatness of the U.S. stock market (see Figure 3.1).

Although rarely reported in the media, something very important has been happening to the value of stocks, as measured by The Dow Jones Industrial Average, since mid 2000: very little. Overall, these stock prices have not only failed to rise, but adjusted for inflation, they have lost value. Given that these Blue Chip stocks remained stable during the Internet Bubble crash, one would expect to see some significant growth since 2000. It didn't happen.

Instead, we've had the worst performing stock market in the world: Dow down 5 percent from its peak in 2000

Figure 3.1   Stock Market Flat Since 2000

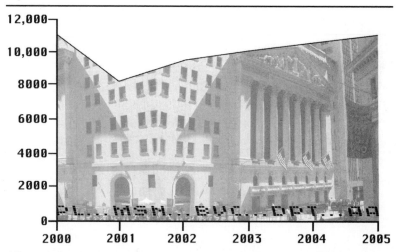

Although the stock market has had its ups and downs since 2000, as of the end of 2005 it is down 5% when adjusted for inflation. This is abysmal performance compared to the 1000% increase in the 20 years prior to 2000.

71

to mid 2006, compared to the Japanese stock market which shot up almost 50 percent in the same period. When adjusted for inflation, the Dow is actually down even more significantly over this time.

Naturally, such tepid performance over such a long period of time, tends to cool investor interest—especially for our oh-so-critical foreign investors, who also face a currency exchange rate risk. The longer our stock market remains in no-grow or slow-growth mode, the more damaging an effect it will have on long-term investor psychology.

Wait a Minute! Can't a No-Growth or Slow-Growth Stock Market Go on for Years?

Yes, a no-growth or slow-growth stock market absolutely can go on for years—if we didn't already have a bubble.

Japan has managed to maintain its flat stock market for many years, but not when they had a bubble. Back when Japan's Nikkei index was up over 40,000, maintaining a flat stock market proved to be impossible.

We too could maintain slow-growth or no-growth for years . . . if we didn't have a Stock Market Bubble. Remember, current stock prices are overvalued, relative to actual earnings. The Dow has increased more than tenfold in the two decades from 1982 to 2000, without an equal rise in real earnings during that same period. To put this increase into perspective, in the five decades prior to 1980, a time of enormous economic growth in our country, the stock market grew a reasonable 300 percent. Then, in the two decades after 1980, the market shot up a whopping 1,000 percent.

That kind of irrational growth means we have a bubble, and you cannot maintain a bubble indefinitely with no growth or slow growth. Keeping a big fat bubble up in the air, defying economic gravity over a long period of time, takes more excitement than that. Irrational exuberance requires a certain minimum amount of, well . . . exuberance! Like a hot air balloon, the current stock market needs a fairly steady supply of heat to keep it up. If it stays too cool for too long, our Stock Market Bubble will become increasingly vulnerable to any downward tug.

What Could Push the Lackluster Stock Market Down? Two Forces: Falling Real Estate and a Declining Dollar

If everything else was fine, we could probably make our overvalued Stock Market Bubble hover in the air, going neither up or down, for many more years. At this particular moment in time, however, we happen to have two other simultaneous financial factors putting downward pressure on the stock market.

In the near term, the slow collapse of the Real Estate Bubble (in some markets, it won't be so slow) will weigh heavily on the stock market. The loss of housing construction jobs, plus the factory and service jobs that support housing construction, will further slow the economy, putting more downward pressure on the stock market (see Figures 3.2).

The mildly declining Dollar Bubble is also putting downward pressure on the stock market. Declines in the U.S. dollar relative to the euro don't inspire tremendous confidence in the overall U.S. economy or the U.S. stock market. Efforts by the Federal Reserve to maintain the

Figure 3.2   Economy Very Dependent on New Housing Jobs

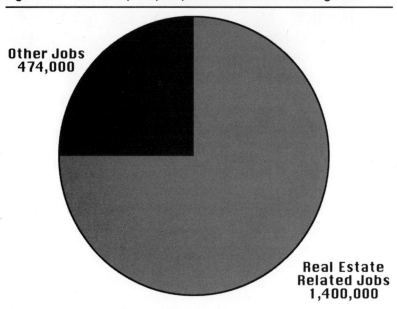

Other Jobs
474,000

Real Estate
Related Jobs
1,400,000

An astounding 74% of ALL new jobs created from the forth quarter of 2000 to the forth quarter of 2005 were related to the housing boom, according to the Bureau of Labor Statistics, including real estate and mortgage brokers, construction workers, architects, building supplies workers and sellers, etc. A major slow down in housing will significantly harm the U.S. economy.

value of the dollar by raising interest rates will help attract foreign investors, but make money more expensive for home mortgages (see Figure 3.3), U.S. businesses, and individuals to borrow. The stock market doesn't like higher interest rates. So as the dollar continues to slip and interests rates rise, the value of U.S. stocks will slip, as well.

Eventually, as the Stock Market Bubble declines toward 8,000, overall investor confidence in the U.S. economy will also decline. Waning foreign investor confidence in U.S. stocks, bonds, real estate, and the dollar, coupled

Figure 3.3 30-Year Mortgage Rates Temporarily Lower Than Short-term Home Equity Rates—That means 30-Year Rates Certain to Go Much Higher

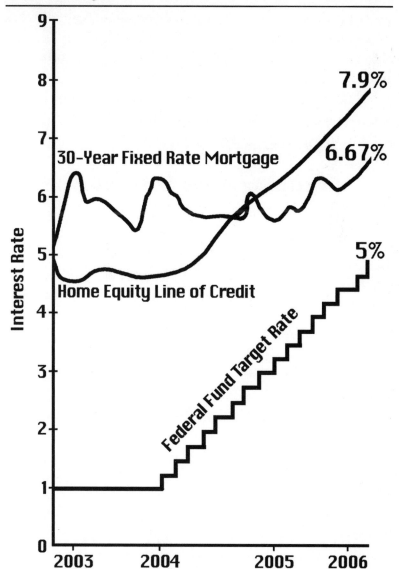

As of Spring 2006, you could borrow for 30 years for almost 1½% LESS than you could borrow for just a few years. This is a very usual phenomenon and cannot last. Soon, 30-year mortgage rates will have to rise to their norm of being 1½% to 2% higher than home equity rates. Of course, by that time, home equity rates may be pushed up even further and growing mortgage delinquencies may push them up even further, still. So, by Summer 2007, 30-year mortgage rates are very likely to be nearing 8% and possibly moving toward 10%.

with a pull toward greater profits elsewhere, will all work together to eventually spook the most conservative (pension funds, life insurance, etc.) foreign investors to begin a sell-off of their U.S. stocks and other U.S. assets in a move to safety and a desire for better returns with other investments. This will cause the Dollar Bubble to seriously fall, forcing the rest of our bubbles to burst.

A Falling Dollar Will Pop the Other Bubbles

When the dollar begins significantly to fall, foreign investors obviously will not find buying U.S. stocks, mortgages, government bonds, and other U.S. assets as appealing as they were when the dollar was on the way up. Decreasing demand for U.S. bonds will automatically drive interest rates even higher. Remember, the government can't function too well without a constant flow of loans, so if investor demand for U.S. bonds drops, we certainly are not going to stop selling them. Instead, we will have to make them more attractive by raising interest rates.

Rising interest rates will dramatically drive stock values down even further. Higher interest rates coupled with falling stocks will further depress the economy and the stock market. Rising interest rates will also further deflate the Real Estate Bubble as cheap mortgages disappear, again putting downward pressure on the economy and the stock market. As these bubbles fall, investor psychology will further deteriorate.

Significant withdrawal of foreign money from the United States could force interest rates to climb as high as 20 percent or more.

Currently we spend almost $350 billion a year in interest on our national debt. If interest rates do go higher, which is quite possible due to our enormous dependence on foreign money and a stable dollar, the interest payments could be truly overwhelming. Even if they only rose to where they were in the early 1980s before the bubbles began, which was 18 percent, the amount we pay in interest would skyrocket to nearly $1 trillion a year—almost three times what it is today. The government would find itself in the same situation as an overextended individual or business who can't keep up with their minimum finance charges due to high interest rates.

Because we must make our interest payments on our own national debt, the government will have no choice but to print more money. Increasing the money supply will provide the dollars to service the debt, but it will also trigger the high inflation that will plague the U.S. economy after the bubbles burst.

Higher interest rates also leave consumers far less eager to buy on credit. Together, a falling Dollar Bubble, falling Stock Market Bubble, falling Real Estate Bubble, and falling Consumer Debt Bubble will throw ice water on consumer spending. Our Porterhouse steak lifestyle is going to be replaced with far more modest fare. Few people will be in the mood to buy super-sized stainless steel outdoor grills, complete with all the bells and whistles, just so they can cook a few cheap hot dogs. We will fix our old cars rather than buy new ones, and tighten our belts across the board. As overall consumer spending declines, American businesses and banks will inevitably suffer and many will fail. U.S. consumers and businesses will also buy less from other countries, temporarily slowing many economies around the globe.

A falling dollar will kick off this unhappy global scenario, and the U.S. and other governments will work like banshees to avoid it.

The Fierce Fight to Save the Dollar

Like two great stock manipulators, China and Japan have both done yeoman's service in maintaining the price of the dollar. Together, they have bought a whopping *$1.75 trillion* worth of dollars as of 2005—almost as much as the U.S. government spends in a year—even though Japan's economy is only half the size of the United State's and China's is one-fifth. Even for a nation with an economy as massive as the U.S. economy, buying this much cash would be no small expenditure. How much more can China and Japan afford? And how much more do they want to risk? They do it to save their exports, a powerful motivator to be sure, but there are limits to their power. Even if they wanted to keep it up indefinitely, at some point, they simply won't be able to.

As of this writing, our greatest ally in maintaining the Dollar Bubble is China. China wants and needs the dollar to stay strong in order to continue building their own growing economy. (We import lots of their stuff.) There are, however, only so many dollars China's central bank can buy before it can buy no more. Maybe the task will be passed to our second greatest ally in propping up the Dollar Bubble, the Japanese. However, as of this writing, Japan's central bank has not bought one dollar since March 2004. It is always possible that Japan will jump

"It's just a flesh wound. I got it defending the dollar."

back into the dollar-buying game when China begins to wane, but doing so costs them real money (a few hundred billion dollars a year) and is seen by the Japanese government as an increasingly risky long-term strategy.

At some point, China and Japan will choke on dollars. Even if they want to keep buying, at some point they will simply run out of money to keep buying our dollars. There are only three ways a government can get more money. One is to tax their citizens. This is not too popular. A second way is to borrow the money. The third way governments can get more money is simply to print more. That, of course, creates another problem: inflation.

To the extent that China finances its purchases of

dollars with borrowing (an easier solution than taxes), it runs the risk of "crowding out" other needs for capital and raises interest rates. This can significantly slow down their economy, which they won't want to do. It also makes Chinese government bonds more attractive to private investors relative to American government bonds, thus drawing Chinese money out of dollars and defeating the purpose of borrowing the money to buy dollars in the first place. So there are limits on just how much China can borrow to buy our dollars. Also, such borrowing leaves the Chinese government very vulnerable in the event that a collapse in the dollar occurs.

Even if China or Japan opt to do one or more of these approaches to get more money to buy our dollars so we can keep buying their exports, eventually the negative consequences of printing, taxing, or borrowing more money will catch up with them and they will cry Uncle and quit.

Perhaps Europe will step in and save us. So far, the Europeans have been pitiful players in the prop-up-the-dollar game, buying only $200 billion—barely as much as tiny Taiwan. Clearly, Europe is not as comfortable with the kind of government economic interventions that Japan and especially China are so willing to employ. Government manipulation of financial markets is much more acceptable in China, which is not a free-market democracy, than it is in Japan and Europe, which do have free markets. Beyond their reluctance to manipulate currency, the Europeans may also see efforts to prop up the dollar as a game they will ultimately lose.

In truth, no central bank really wants to buy large quantities of dollars. They only do it because they have to, as a last resort when private investors fail to buy enough to maintain the dollar's price. The fact that China and Japan have felt the need to buy $1.75 trillion in dollars certainly shows that the demand for dollars by private investors is down. Private investors are losing interest in buying our dollars because they are losing confidence in the profit potential of U.S. assets.

How much bigger the gap will get between the number of dollars private investors are willing to buy and what central banks must pick up, we don't know. What we can say for sure is that there is no reason in the world to think private investors will magically change their minds and bail us out. Private investors are motivated by profits. Like any other commodity, dollars are bought and sold in accordance with the laws of supply and demand. With our international Trade Deficit Bubble rising at a rapid rate, more and more of our dollars are flowing out to other countries as we import their goods. A flood of dollars into the hands of business owners in other countries does not increase demand for dollars. Falling demand for dollars due to the huge Trade Deficit Bubble and declining general interest in U.S. stocks and other assets, means fewer private investors have any reason at all to buy dollars.

Instead, foreign investors will want to get rid of some of their dollar assets and put their money into safer investments back in their home countries where they may get the same tepid returns on their government bonds as they are getting on U.S. bonds, but they avoid the risk of a falling dollar. The upside potential of buying their own government's bonds may be limited, but so are the downside risks.

As private investment interest wanes, central banks continue to pick up the slack—at least for a while. As we said, at some point they simply won't be able to. (For more information, see **www.americasbubbleeconomy.com/ centralbanksbuydollars.**)

In the meantime, every dollar China and Japan buy just enlarges our already bloated Dollar Bubble. The bigger the bubble gets, the worse it will be when it pops. The more effort that goes into maintaining the Dollar Bubble, despite economic gravity, the greater will be the pressure to dump overvalued dollars on the way down.

The Bigger the Bubble, the Harder the Fall

There's a big difference between falling off a stepstool in your kitchen and falling off the roof of a 30-floor office building. Obviously, one is going to hurt a whole lot more.

The economic advantages of creating and maintaining multiple bubbles are enormous. The combined effect of an overvalued Stock Market Bubble, an overpriced Dollar Bubble, a booming Real Estate Bubble, and nearly endless loans coming to us via the Consumer Debt Bubble has created breathtaking economic growth for the United States.

On the flipside, the combined economic disadvantages when these bubbles interact, collide, and ultimate fall will be equally breathtaking. One bursting bubble quickly causes others to burst, creating very dramatic and rapid economic decline. Imagine for a moment what life might be like if the dollars in your wallet bought a lot less than they do now, your home value significantly falls, the stock market takes a real hit, and consumer spending takes a nosedive. Not exactly the recipe for booming prosperity.

Keeping all our bubbles up in the air, and keeping them from colliding and pulling each other down, is a very delicate balancing act. Like a start-up company with a fast burn rate, every day the U.S. economy needs a great deal of cash. The last time we checked, the federal government was adding to it's already incomprehensible debt at the rate of about *$7 billion a week*. So, we desperately need foreign investors and we need to keep our foreign investors very, very happy. But as our bubbles begin to collide, it gets harder and harder to keep investor capital flowing in. When a business in constant need of cash begins to have troubles in some areas, such as product development or marketing, it gets harder and harder to get investors to pony up. It's not the troubles themselves that directly kill the company; it's the loss of investor confidence that ultimately pulls the plug.

Unlike a startup company, the American economy has had a long history of prosperity and solid financial success, especially prior to our borrowing spree beginning in 1982. Our bubbles may be relatively new, but our deep wealth has been with us for quite sometime. Like a wealthy family fallen on bad times, we can use our many resources to postpone the pain. In addition to our power and wealth, America will use its ability to deny the facts and keep going as if nothing is wrong. Big bubbles, coupled with big American expectations that things can only get better, will make for a very long, very painful fall when foreign investor psychology turns negative and the bubbles pop.

What's the Best Analogy for Our Bubble Economy? Is It the Internet Stock Bubble? The Florida Land Boom? No, Believe It or Not, It's Enron!

Few people had a clue that one of the largest U.S. companies, built on one of the most solid U.S. assets— natural gas pipelines—was about to go under. Was it really so hard to see that Enron was actually a house of cards headed for a fall?

How is it possible that so many Enron accountants (the most esteemed in the nation), lawyers (the most esteemed in Houston), investment bankers (the most esteemed in the world), stockholders, employees, and managers all simultaneously suffered group blindness in the face of the facts: Enron's basic business practices were a disaster waiting to happen, and anyone with their eyes open could have easily seen it.

The truth is, everyone involved was smart enough to see it coming, they just didn't want to. Management may have been guilty of misleading people, but that doesn't change the fact that everyone desperately wanted to be misled.

Ironically, Enron's motto was, "Ask Why." Apparently, no one ever did. And the same is true of America's bubble economy. Like the Enron folks who had so much to gain by keeping their eyes closed, America seems to be suffering simultaneous bubble blindness.

Before Enron collapsed, no one asked why their stock was up 50 percent in just one year and then up almost 100 percent the next. No one asked why Enron stock jumped up 30 percent in just a few days, following a relatively minor announcement that they would enter a new broadband market. No, nobody asked. They all just kept quiet and kept making money. Despite the plain facts, they all desperately wanted to believe the good times would never end.

Just like the rest of us.

Along the same line of thinking regarding the U.S. economy, is it really that hard to see that $8 trillion in government debt that can't possibly be paid back might not be the best thing for the country? Is it really that hard to see the fallacy in homes appreciating 80 percent while incomes are up only 2 percent? Is it really that hard to see that the stock market is overvalued when it's up more that 1,000 percent in 20 years without an equal rise in real earnings? And why isn't anyone mentioning the disturbing fact that China and Japan have had to buy almost $2 trillion of our U.S. dollars just to prop up its value? Is it really that difficult to see that all this, coupled with a nearly $1 trillion trade deficit, might be setting us up for one hell of a fall?

The Two Great Motivators, Fear and Greed, Will Accelerate the Fall

Most bubbles pop because investors fear loss of money. In this case, the demise of the bubbles will be driven by both fear and greed—fear of losing money on their U.S. investments and the ability to make huge amounts of money in other investments. That is a powerful combination. It's as if investors will be pushed and pulled by two giant magnets. On one side, they will be pushed away from their U.S. assets because of falling asset values that limit or eliminate profits. Investors don't like that. On the other side, investors will be strongly pulled toward the irresistible prospect of making huge profits elsewhere, primarily in euros and gold. Investors very much like that.

Both these magnets—the fear of loss and the desire for gain—will push or pull investors to unload their U.S. investments.

The "Fear Factor": The Fear of Losing Money

The fear of losing money will be a major motivator for investors to sell their U.S. assets. The more people sell, the lower asset values will fall and the more people will want to sell, further depressing prices.

Two things will help push this fear along. The first and most important is the growing dissatisfaction with the American government and economy. Foreigners invest in the United States, not only because the returns have been so good, but also because they draw comfort from the feeling that the United States is well managed and rock solid. Once foreigners begin to perceive the United States as poorly led or less than bulletproof, psychology turns more negative. This is where intangible factors, like the war in Iraq, could have an impact. Unfavorable views of the Iraq war—either because we got in it in the first place or because it's going on much longer than we anticipated—is already tarnishing the U.S. image abroad. With less confidence in the United States and its government, foreigners become less interested in investing. Other factors, such as a slowdown in economic growth and declining real incomes may also undermine our "rock-solid" image with both foreign and domestic investors.

Another factor that may push things along is the fear of what the U.S. Federal Reserve may do next. In particular investors may become more anxious in the absence of Alan Greenspan. Whatever people might say about Greenspan's tenure as Federal Reserve Chairman, few would deny his ability to produce a certain amount of confidence among investors, both foreign and domestic. Maintaining this confidence becomes more and more critical as people begin seeing warning signs of problems with the dollar, the housing market, and the stock market. Greenspan had a knack for putting investors at ease, even in the face of obvious dangers. He didn't always ignore

Source: cartoonstock.com

dangers, but he tended to downplay them in a way that made investors feel more comfortable. By doing so, he either purposely or not so purposely, had a significant role in allowing our various bubbles to grow so large.

In Greenspan's absence, the bubbles will be harder to maintain. It's not that the new Federal Reserve Chairman, Ben Bernanke, will be particularly bad. So far, he's gotten a decent reception from investors; and in terms of movements in the overnight Fed Funds Rate, Bernanke may make very similar decisions to what Greenspan would have done. However, when problems appear, few people are better than Greenspan at maintaining positive psychology. As our multiple bubbles collide, Greenspan's absence may hasten their collapse.

In addition to these two "fear factors," there's an even more compelling reason why foreign investors will eventually want to dump dollars . . .

The "Greed Factor": The Irresistible Pull of Huge Profits Elsewhere

Usually when a bubble pops, the best you can hope for is to get out early enough to keep your shirt. Certainly, with the Tulip Bubble, the 1929 Stock Market Crash, and the Internet Bubble, there was precious little good news for anyone involved. If you managed to sell before prices dropped too low, great. But, there was no way to benefit from the actual bursting of these bubbles.

With our current set of interactive bubbles, things are much different. Unlike bubbles before, the bursting of our current bubbles will offer individuals a truly golden opportunity to make money—*lots and lots of money*. The primal investor desire to protect assets and the primal investor desire to increase wealth combine to accelerate the mad dash out of dollars and other U.S. assets, and into other lucrative investments, particularly gold and euros. We have much, much more to say about how you can tap into this bonanza of potential profits in Chapter 5, Cashing in on Chaos. Right now it's important to understand that both fear and greed drive the action.

Gold has a special attraction for foreign investors, particularly Asian and Middle Eastern. If gold continues to perform as it has for the past few years—and all the fundamentals indicate that it will—foreign investors will want to divert some of their dollar investments into gold. In fact, even some central banks are already considering doing so.

Gold is an increasingly attractive investment for American investors, as well. No longer dismissed as merely the obsession of "gold bugs," gold is gaining serious respect as more and more mainstream investors join in. Part of the shift in acceptability of gold has been the development of *Exchange Traded Funds* (ETFs), which makes it easy to invest in gold. Financial advisors at major brokerage firms are beginning to recommend putting a small part of one's portfolio, up to 10 percent, in gold as a "hedge against inflation." The fact that gold has increased nearly 120 percent and the Dow has lost almost 5 percent (NASDAQ down almost 50 percent) since 2000, makes gold much more than merely an inflation hedge, especially for foreign investors who general have a stronger interest in gold than Americans (see Figure 3.4).

Converting dollars to euros will also be quite profitable. Although investments in euros took a small beating in 2005, Warren Buffet, America's most famous euro investor, is right: In the long term, euros are a good alternative investment for Americans and foreigners, alike. With continued pressure from the huge Trade Deficit Bubble, it is doubtful that the dollar can continue its yearlong comeback. The rise in 2005 was due in large part to the many interest rate hikes by the Fed. But, continued rate hikes will hurt the economy and the Fed is likely to back off. At the same time, the European Central Bank has shown a willingness to increase its interest rates, making euros even more attractive. At the time of this writing, the dollar is still down 35 percent from its peak against the euro.

Won't Our Government Try to Save the Economy?

You bet! In fact, they are trying to do that right now. How? The old-fashioned way: they continue to borrow lots of money, of course! Nothing beats a nice, fat, foreign-funded

Figure 3.4   Gold Up, Stocks Down

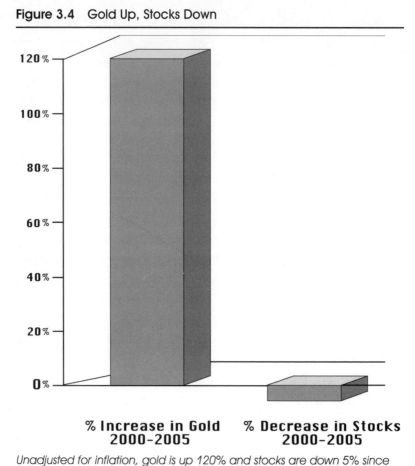

% Increase in Gold **% Decrease in Stocks**
2000-2005   **2000-2005**

Unadjusted for inflation, gold is up 120% and stocks are down 5% since 2000. Gold is clearly in a solid bull market and will likely lure more investors away from stock.

government deficit for curing all economic ills—in the short term.

No one would argue with this. If the question was put squarely to economists, most liberals and conservatives alike would agree that there is simply no more powerful an engine for job creation and economic growth than a big foreign-funded government deficit. Domestically funded government deficits are far less desirable because they can quickly harm the economy by forcing interest rates to soar when the government tries to grab cash from the domestic economy alone. But a foreign-funded deficit is practically a gift from heaven.

In the short term, there are no downsides. In the short term, foreign-funded deficits keep the economy going and growing, and all our bubbles nicely pumped. In the short term, Vice President Dick Cheney is right when he said, "Reagan showed us that deficits don't matter." Deficit spending massively contributes to economic growth—in the short term.

There's only one problem. The short term does not last forever.

Can't We Just Keep Running Bigger and Bigger Foreign-Funded Deficits and Save the Economy?

Sounds great, but in reality, it can't happen. Without a solid, real economic foundation to support all that growth, sooner or later, economic gravity kicks in and what goes up must come down. In the long term, the dollar will fall, foreigners will balk and leave, and our big, fat foreign-funded Government Deficit Bubble—along with the rest of America's Bubble Economy—will pop.

Nonetheless, in the short term, we can—and probably will—run big deficits to keep all our bubbles up in the air a little longer. Of course, if we're still running a large Government Deficit Bubble when the other bubbles collide (and there's no reason to think we won't), the impact will be even more devastating for our economy.

Remember: the bigger the bubble, the harder the fall.

When Will the Bubbles Burst?

If there's one golden rule about when bubbles collide and burst, it is that it takes longer than anyone might anticipate; but it hits far harder and the effects last much longer than anyone would anticipate. Many people naturally want to maintain (and enlarge) a bubble as long as possible because there are so many benefits to keeping it going and so terrible a cost to letting it burst.

Trying to predict precisely when America's bubble economy will burst is like trying to nail down Jello. Again and again, just when it looks like the crisis is almost upon us, our economy seems to spring back to life. The most likely scenario, detailed below, involves the rapid removal of foreign capital and the rapid fall of the value of the dollar on the foreign exchange market, most likely in the next two to five years. Deficit spending may delay it longer, but probably no later than 2012. Or the bubbles could pop sooner if investor confidence continues to wane. It could happen all at once or in small increments leading up to a final plunge. (For more details, see **www.americasbubbleeconomy.com/timing.**)

The lower the level of investor confidence, the less of a trigger that is needed to set things off. Low confidence, combined with any sort of bad news, could start the stampede of both foreign and American investors out of the United States like rats fleeing a sinking ship.

Trouble overseas, such as a Japanese banking collapse, could also set things off, as it did when the fall of an Austrian bank helped trigger the Great Depression by collapsing German banks, which, in turn, weakened U.S. banks and burst our speculative stock market bubble in 1929. Even an overseas boom could prompt investors to begin removing money from the U.S. stock market and placing it elsewhere.

Anything that causes foreign investors to begin pulling their money out of the United States in a flight to safety in their own currencies is the beginning of the end. Once the rush begins, nothing will stop investors from rushing off to make huge profits by selling off dollars and their other U.S. assets.

How to Keep the Party Going—For a While

We have five short-term fixes for keeping America's Bubble Economy temporarily afloat. Of course, postponing the inevitable only makes our bubbles bigger and fall harder when they do pop, but in the short run, we can keep the party going a bit longer. How many of the following do you think we will actually do? Keep an eye out; it will be interesting.

1. *Increase the Federal Government deficit.* The most powerful boost to the economy from an increased deficit comes from cutting taxes or increased spending. A growing deficit due to declining taxes from a falling economy will do us little good. What we'll need is to cut taxes or raise spending, or both. The limit is that at some point, the government will borrow so much, that we spook foreign and domestic investors and the Bubblequake may begin.

2. *Increase interest rates.* This is the most powerful tool for attracting foreign money into the United States. The limit is raising interest rates so high that it hurts the economy and stock market. That will turn foreign investors off.

3. *Encourage China, Japan and other foreign governments to buy dollars.* We can't be too obvious about this or we will spook foreign and domestic investors, but whatever we can do to get foreign governments to buy more and more dollars, the better. The limit is that someday China, Japan, and other foreign governments won't be able to keep it up forever. At some point, they will stop buying, the Dollar Bubble will fall, and investors will fly out of their U.S. assets.

4. *Create another Internet Bubble.* This is hard to do since it depends so heavily on investor psychology, but if we can somehow get investors incredibly excited about something new, maybe nanotechnology, that could set off another stock-buying frenzy. The limit is, if it's a bubble, at some point what goes up, must come down. At this point, it might trigger a much broader drop in the stock market.

5. *Restart the Housing Boom.* Lowering interest rates could hold up the Real Estate Bubble. Only problem is we need to keep interest rates up so we can attract foreign investors to buy our government bonds, so we can keep running the country on borrowed money. Right now, that's more important than restarting the housing boom. Oh, what a tangled economy we weave when we practice to deceive—ourselves.

Bubblequake: A Two-Stage Collapse— at First Very Slowly and Then Very, Very Fast

Mark Twain once said, when asked how he went bankrupt, "At first very slowly, and then, very quickly." We have every reason to believe that is exactly how our bubbles will pop.

Stage One (Very Slowly)

Step 1. A change in long-term investor confidence in the stock market due to years of little or no growth, declining real estate values, rising interest rates, mild declines in the dollar, a rise in gold as an alternative investment especially for foreigners, and a slowing U.S. economy. No panic, just a general malaise. (All this is already happening.)

Step 2. Slow decline in the stock market to the 8,000 range (Dow Jones) over a period of a couple of years.

Step 3. With the stock market at 8,000, the pressures on the Dollar Bubble will mount. Private investors will be less willing to buy dollars due to the lackluster stock market and the overall economy, plus growing concern about those big foreign-funded government deficits we talked about. As private investors step away from the dollar, the central banks will feel pressured to step in. China (and perhaps Japan and others) will increase their dollar purchases.

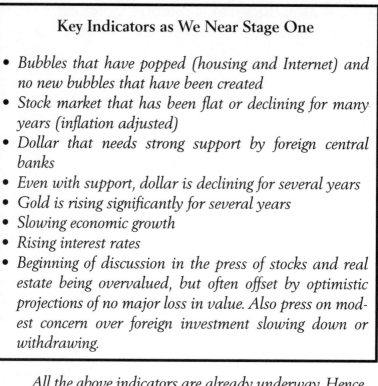

Key Indicators as We Near Stage One

- *Bubbles that have popped (housing and Internet) and no new bubbles that have been created*
- *Stock market that has been flat or declining for many years (inflation adjusted)*
- *Dollar that needs strong support by foreign central banks*
- *Even with support, dollar is declining for several years*
- *Gold is rising significantly for several years*
- *Slowing economic growth*
- *Rising interest rates*
- *Beginning of discussion in the press of stocks and real estate being overvalued, but often offset by optimistic projections of no major loss in value. Also press on modest concern over foreign investment slowing down or withdrawing.*

All the above indicators are already underway. Hence, we are nearing Stage One. If the trends slow down, expect Stage One to last longer, if the trends speed up, expect Stage One to be shorter.

Stage Two (Very Fast)

After two to five years in stressful Stage One, the second stage of our multiple bubble collapse is likely to occur very, very quickly—probably within a matter of months. Here's one possible way the dominoes will fall:

Step 1. With long term psychology now significantly changed, foreign investor skittishness about U.S.

assets turns into outright nervousness. The most conservative foreign investors (life insurance companies, pension funds, banks, etc.) move to reduce their exposure in American stocks and bonds. They don't panic, they just feel that the small gains to be had by buying U.S. securities, which in the case of stocks have recently become losses, are more than offset by the risk of a falling dollar. Because they are required to be conservative in their investments, they have to be extra careful.

Step 2. This outflow of money reduces stock prices even further and causes more selling by both American and foreign investors, who have become disenchanted with the lukewarm to negative returns they have been getting for almost a decade. They see little upside potential in the stock market and some significant downside. At least back home they don't have to risk that their meager stock or real estate gains will be wiped out by a declining dollar.

Step 3. Increasingly, investors are turning to gold and euros, which are both doing quite well by this point, providing additional incentives to leave the stock market.

Step 4. With the stock market declining, housing markets down, and the economy slowing, the government suddenly finds itself dealing with far less tax revenue. This creates a large budget deficit, this time with far less foreign capital coming into the United States to compensate for this deficit.

Step 5. To entice money from a smaller pool of investor dollars, the government is forced to raise interest rates. Higher interest rates depress the capital goods sector: homes, home furnishings, large appliances, automobiles, factories, office buildings, and large equipment. Falling sales leads to higher unemployment, further slowing the economy.

Step 6. Despite interest rate hikes, there is still not enough foreign capital to meet the government's needs, leaving the Federal Reserve no choice but to print more money to finance the deficit and boost the economy. This causes higher inflation.

Step 7. The combination of soaring interest rates and high inflation sends stock values even lower. A stock's value is based on discounted earnings, which means that returns to shareholders have to be more than the inflated interest rates that they could get from government bonds or treasury bills. Stock prices go up due to inflation, but their real value declines. The Stock Market Bubble is bursting.

Step 8. Central banks, which have been buying up dollars to prevent a collapse, sustain massive losses in their investments and are unable and/or unwilling to continue to intervene. The world's Chief Dollar Manipulator, China, eventually runs out of cash to buy dollars, or at least feels enough economic stress to reduce their purchases. The Dollar Bubble is bursting.

Step 9. At this point, investors enter a period of "Rational Panic." The sooner and faster an investor sells dollars and dollar investments, the better off that investor will be. It is a panic, but it is quite rational because selling at whatever price the investor can get is absolutely the right thing to do.

Step 10. A falling dollar and downwardly spiraling stock market leads to more panic in the foreign exchange market, causing a further collapse in the value of the dollar and more decline in the stock and bond markets. At the same time, the U.S. government is trying to figure out how to pay the interest on a debt that has now skyrocketed. The Government Deficit Bubble is bursting.

Step 11. High interest rates (20 percent or higher due to lack of foreign capital that was keeping interest rates low earlier) are killing real estate values across the country, not just in "frothy" areas. The Real Estate Bubble is bursting.

Step 12. High interest rates also hurt credit card companies. The combination of customers not making their payments, plus the high rates these companies must pay for capital, forces them to go bankrupt fairly quickly, greatly reducing the amount of credit card credit available. What credit is available, many people don't want to touch at the high interest rates the card companies will need to charge to cover the cost of funds and their losses (40 percent plus). Consumer spending hits record lows. The Consumer Debt Bubble is bursting.

Step 13. A falling dollar also means the price of imported goods skyrockets. This is Adam Smith's "invisible hand" at work, forcing world trade back into equilibrium by adjusting exchange rates. We greatly reduce our imports. The Trade Deficit Bubble is bursting.

Step 14. America's Bubble Economy collapses, impacting the entire globe.

Step 15. China, Japan and Europe, heavily dependent on income from their exports to the United States, find the American crash cascading into a crash of their own economies.

Step 16. This hurts countries as such as Indonesia, Taiwan, Korea, and Brazil who supplied many of the raw materials or finished goods to China and Japan.

Step 17. Spectacular profits are made by reasonable people who face facts early and position themselves to cash in on what will be one of the biggest transfers of wealth in human history. (To join them, please see Chapters 5 through 7.)

Key Indicators as We Near Stage Two:

- *Stock market falls into the 7000–9000 range*
- *The dollar falls into the $0.50–$0.70 range, relative to the euro*
- *30 year mortgage rates rise to the 10–12% range*
- *Price of gold tops $1000 per ounce*
- *Growing pessimism about future economic growth in the United States.*
- *A lot of discussion in the press about stocks and real estate being overvalued. Also significant press on a possible rapid withdrawal of a large amount of assets from the United States by foreign investors.*

Is There Any Way to Limit the Damage Once It Pops?

The only way to limit the impact of so many falling bubbles, is to purposely pop the bubbles early before things get any worse—starting with purposely devaluing the dollar. That's about as likely to happen as a criminal turning himself in early to get a jump on his jail time. No one wants to face the music, so the only other option is to put the inevitable off for as long as possible by continuing to run big foreign-funded government deficits each year. It's the all-purpose Super Power Pill of the modern U.S. economy. Works every time.

However, once foreign investor psychology radically sours in Stage Two, all government attempts to keep America's Bubble Economy afloat will ultimately fail. The dollar will significantly fall, along with all the other bubbles. Inflation and interest rates will climb, American consumers will be in a state of shock, and the U.S. economy— along with every other economy that depends on us—will settle into 10 years or more of global mega-recession.

Why so long?

Because it took a long, long time to create these bubbles and so the after effects of their demise will not clear quickly. Unlike the Internet Bubble, which went up and down relatively fast and did not interact much with the rest of the economy, any bubble crash that involves the fall of the U.S. dollar is going to have a deep and wide impact. How could it not?

Until then, the value of the dollar will continue to "depend on the kindness of strangers." Right now, that means the Chinese. In a few years, that might mean the

Chinese and the Japanese, and perhaps even some others. But the kind of "kindness" we need will cost staggeringly large amounts of money, and it won't be long before there simply are no kind strangers left.

China, Japan, and other nations cannot keep buying dollars forever. When the dollar begins to significantly fall, foreign investors will want out as quickly as possible—and they will stay out for quite a while.

Won't the Falling Dollar Immediately Attract Foreign Investors Back into the United States?

Under more normal conditions, that would make sense. Unfortunately in this situation, the answer is no. Foreign investors are not going to rush back into the United States. Why? Because there will have been a fundamental shift in the value of U.S. assets.

Did investors immediately rush back into the stock market after the 1929 crash? Did investors immediately rush back in to buy Internet stocks after the Internet Bubble popped in 2000? Of course they didn't because the fundamentals had changed. Eventually, investors did return to the stock market, and in time, foreign money will return to the United States. But in the short term, they are not going to run back.

Think about the U.S. economy like an individual company. If an individual company's stock falls quite low there is only one reason to rush in and buy it: you believe in its future potential growth because its fundamental value is there, based on rational economic factors. In the case of the United States, immediately after the dollar falls and the rest of the bubbles pop, there is no immediate reason to believe in fundamental value. Long-term, the United States certainly has the potential of coming back, but in the immediate future, following the pop, few investors will want to put their money where there is no fundamental value and won't be for quite a while.

Even if the assets of other nations are less profitable than assets in the United States, most foreign investors are unlikely to return to the United States any time soon. They will worry about losing whatever profit they can make on our assets when they convert their shrinking dollars into their own currencies. The risk of a significantly falling dollar will offset the hope of a profit on their dollar-denominated investments.

The bottom line is, if the U.S. dollar is not strong, no other U.S. assets will be all that appealing, especially when investors can make so much money on rising euros and gold.

And the good news is, so can you (see Chapter 5 and 6).

Five Ways to Track Our Bubble Troubles

1. Foreign-owned U.S. Assets

The higher this number, the harder it will be to cope with the removal of foreign capital. Currently, foreign investors own an astronomical $12 trillion of U.S. assets, including dollars, stocks, bonds, real estate, and more. As more and more U.S. assets are in the hands of foreign investors, only a smaller and smaller percentage has to move out to destabilize the U.S. economy.

2. **Ratio of Foreign-owned U.S. Assets to the U.S. Money Supply (M_1)**

The higher this ratio, the less power our Federal Reserve has to react to the removal of foreign capital. In our view, anything over 2 is potentially dangerous. Currently, this ratio is a whopping 12.

3. **U.S. Government Debt**

A big foreign-funded government deficit makes us vulnerable to the future actions of foreign investors. Currently, the U.S. deficit stands at an astronomical $8 trillion.

4. **Dollar Purchases by Foreign Central Banks**

The central banks of foreign countries step in to buy dollars when private investors lose interest. The lower private investor confidence, the more central banks have to buy dollars to artificially prop up its price. As of 2005, China and Japan have bought $1.75 trillion worth of U.S. dollars.

5. **Falling Asset Values**

- In mid 2005, U.S. stocks were down 5 percent since the peak in 2000 . After adjusted for inflation, the loss is even greater.
- In the last five years, the dollar fell 35 percent from its peak against the euro.
- Home prices are rising modestly or falling in some places, compared to double digit growth in the previous 5 years.

For updated information about these and other important economic indicators, please visit **www .americasbubbleeconomy.com/indicators.**

Chapter FOUR

What!? You Mean We're Not King of the World!?

Frequently Asked Questions About How It Really <u>Can</u> Happen Here

If you've read this far—and apparently, you have—that can only mean one of two things: Either you think we are right on target and you can't wait to see what we say next, or you are a bit skeptical (okay, very skeptical). Nevertheless, you are willing to give us one more chapter of your valuable time to see if we can answer some of your most pressing questions. Either way, we thank you.

Now, to your burning questions . . .

If things really are that bad, why is the economy doing so well? You doom-and-gloomers are always predicting disaster. Haven't you noticed that it never actually happens?

We are definitely *not* doom-and-gloomers. But you are right, economic pessimists often do say that disaster is just around the corner and then, corner after corner, no disaster actually befalls us. Many years later, when something unusually negative does happen to occur, the pessimists love to jump up and down and brag that they saw it coming.

It reminds us of that old joke about the chronic hypochondriac who spent his whole life insisting he was near death. Finally, after passing away at the ripe old age of 102, his tombstone read: "I told you I was sick!"

Forget the permanent pessimists, and forget their close cousins, the perpetually perky. Smart, reasonable people don't make up their minds based on fantasy dreams or dire nightmares. Smart, reasonable people focus on reality, so let's quickly review the facts:

- We know our *dollar is overvalued* because the Chinese and Japanese have bought $1.75 trillion of our dollars to prop up the price.

- We know our *stocks are overvalued* because the Dow has increased 10-fold in 20 years, without an equal rise in real earnings.

- We know our *real estate is overvalued* because personal incomes and population growth have not increased at the same pace.

- We know we have *too much consumer debt* compared to our incomes and our near-zero saving rate.

- We know we have *astronomical government debt*, now at more than $8 trillion and growing, and this debt is heavily funded by foreign capital.

- We know we have a *gigantic international trade* deficit, nearing $1 trillion annually.

We also know there is nothing significant happening right now in the United States to jump start our economy with huge productivity improvements or stunning new technologies that the rest of the world can only buy from us.

The U.S. economy is currently a collection of bubbles, and you needn't be a doom-and-gloom pessimist to believe in gravity. What goes up, must come down. It's that simple.

The reason the bubbles haven't popped yet is also simple: They still contain a lot of hot air—people still want to believe in them.

China and Japan certainly want to believe. They need U.S. consumers to keep buying their exports to keep their own economies going. That's why China and Japan have

"Up a hundred and sixteen points! If only we'd had the foresight to invest ten minutes ago."

spent $1.75 trillion of their own money to buy our dollars. They want a nice, strong U.S. dollar, even if they have to pay good money for it.

U.S. investors who currently own U.S. stocks, bonds, and real estate certainly want to believe, too. And of course, the U.S. government wants to maintain a nice, strong dollar so foreign investors will keep buying U.S. bonds, lending us the gazillions of dollars we need to keep the party going. Everyone naturally wants to keep America's Bubble Economy afloat for a very, very long time. Forever would be ideal. But sooner or later, our collection of bubbles will inevitably collide and burst—most likely beginning with a volatile stock market.

How in the world can anyone in their right mind possibly say that the U.S. stock market is in a bubble?

Many people believe that because stock values have remained steady since the Internet Bubble crash in 2000, it means there is no reason to think we have a bubble in the market. They say we've already had our "correction" (Internet stock crash) and now all is well.

While it's true that the NASDAQ is down more than 50 percent from its peak, the Dow is only down about 5 percent from its peak, so there's still a lot of irrational value left there. Remember, the Dow rose tenfold in the last 20 years, compared to only a threefold increase in the previous 50 years (see Figure 4.1).

Even after the Internet crash, the NASDAQ is still up almost twelvefold in 20 years. Most of this growth is due to huge foreign investment in U.S. bonds, which drove interest rates down. Falling interest rates drove stock values up.

Figure 4.1   Irrational Exuberance

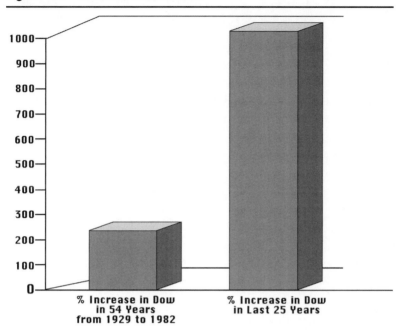

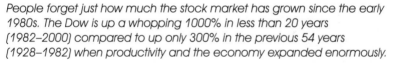

People forget just how much the stock market has grown since the early 1980s. The Dow is up a whopping 1000% in less than 20 years (1982–2000) compared to up only 300% in the previous 54 years (1928–1982) when productivity and the economy expanded enormously.

Rising stock values further pumped up our booming economy, already juiced up on lots of foreign-funded government debt, low interest rates, and a housing and consumer credit boom. Bubbles do beget bubbles.

More recently, from mid 2000 to 2005, the stock market has been stalled in a state many money managers like to call "stable"—which is really just a euphemism for pathetic performance. Nobody wants to say it quite that bluntly, but that's how everyone really feels. Market boosters tell us to just wait out this period of pathetic performance and eventually stock growth will reappear. They say there may be no immediate upside; but there's also no significant downside risk. So just relax until the upside returns.

Of course, the idea that the stock market at any time is risk-free is completely false. Every market has downside risk. Back in the 1950s, '60s, and '70s, that was completely understood. It's been a very long time since the experts have tried to tell us there's no risk in the stock market. Guess when it happened before? The last time market cheerleaders tried to get Americans to think of the stock market as risk-free was just before the big 1929 stock market crash that led to the Great Depression. Coincidence?

A bloated, overvalued market (Dow up tenfold in 20 years), now "stable" from mid 2000 to 2005 (also know as stagnant), plus cheerleaders telling us there's no downside risk, all add up to one thing: a Stock Market Bubble on the edge (see Figure 4.2).

Figure 4.2   Hockey Stick Dow

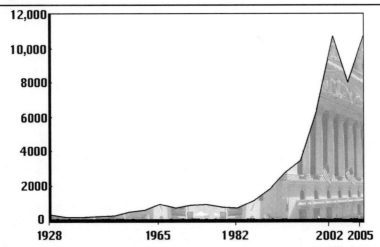

Since 1928, the Dow has grown like a hockey stick (flat, then sharply up). What was so different about the last two decades years compared to the three decades before that?

If the U.S. economy is so terrible, why are so many people and businesses making so much money?

Good question. Simple answer: Bubbles are quite profitable—before they burst. By definition, a rising bubble is a rising asset value, primarily based on rising perceived value (rather than real, rock-solid, economic growth). Can you make money on a rising bubble? You bet you can! In fact, that's precisely why it rises. Can individuals and businesses also make money in a more-or-less stable bubble, one that's neither rising nor falling? Absolutely.

So the fact that people and businesses are making lots of money right now certainly does not prove that the U.S. economy is bubble-free.

Currently, our bubble economy is relatively stable, propped up by a combination of several, linked, interdependent bubbles, each holding the others up. Conversely, when these bubbles begin to seriously collide and fall, each will drag the others down. In the meantime, plenty of money can and will be made.

As things progress, you will want to stay smart, reasonable, and alert. Don't allow yourself to be swayed by people who desperately want you to keep buying whatever it is they are selling.

Why Don't More Economists Measure the Enormous Stimulative Effect of the Federal Deficit?

Despite having been through 25 years of the greatest economic experiment of our times—stimulating the U.S. economy with huge government deficit spending— surprisingly little economic research is done on the topic. Yes, there has been massive research about the federal deficit; but very little of it focuses on how much the deficit directly boosts the economy and indirectly boosts U.S. asset values. Certainly, this is an obvious and important economic issue that deserves serious investigation.

It's almost as if economists would rather not look too closely at how much of our economic growth over the past 25 years has resulted from government stimulation through deficit spending. Could there be a bit of denial here, even among economists? In fairness, this kind of analysis is outside of most economists' specific areas of expertise.

Still, it's an interesting question. Why so little research?

Doesn't the economy run in cycles? Isn't this just a temporary downturn that will cycle back to an upturn soon?

Under more normal conditions, thinking in terms of economic cycles makes sense. In a stable system, there are natural ups and downs within predictable limits. During this unique time, however, we have very little routine economics going on. Instead, we have an unusual convergence of several simultaneous bubbles, including a tower of government debt ($8 trillion) and a huge amount of foreign-owned U.S. assets ($12 trillion).

It's safe to say our economy has never been in these circumstances before, and with any luck we will never, ever be again. Nothing about the current situation is routine and so all the usual economic cycle arguments simply do not apply.

Few people are willing to expose any of this, especially in the mainstream media. One notable exception is *Newsweek*'s Robert Samuelson, one of the few mainstream financial writers willing to take on the conventional wisdom and reveal some of the underlying realities of today's economy. For someone whose audience is not always that comfortable with hearing the truth, Samuelson has shown an unusual amount of courage, honest analysis, and foresight. While Samuelson certainly does not agree with all we say, he is one of the best mainstream financial writers out there today and always well worth reading.

Why all the hand-wringing about so much foreign-owned U.S. assets? Doesn't the fact that so many foreigners want to buy our stocks, bonds, and other assets prove we are the greatest economy on earth?

On the surface, this question really does seem to make a lot of sense. Obviously, foreign investors chose to buy our stocks, bonds, dollars, real estate, and other U.S. assets in order to make a profit. And if they kept coming back to buy more and more of our assets, then the profits must have been pretty darn good. Foreigners have, in fact, done extremely well with their U.S. investments for the last 25 years.

But if returns remain flat for too much longer, then they will start leaving in droves—it's as simple as that. Foreign investors are in it for the money, not for love of our country. As long as we can give them outstanding returns, we have nothing to worry about. But, as those mutual fund commercials always warn "past performance is no guarantee of future performance."

Future performance will not likely be anywhere near as good as in the past. Meager returns, coupled with fear of a falling dollar, eventually drive foreigners away. And once they finally go, they go faster than they came. Massive

Source: cartoonstock.com

foreign investment isn't a bad thing in and of itself. It's massive foreign *disinvestment* that is going to be quite bad. Because we have taken in so much foreign investment and because it has been so key to our economic growth over the last 25 years (keeping interest rates, inflation low, and stocks booming stock market), the U.S. economy is now extremely vulnerable to the withdrawal of that investment.

Why would foreign investors ever leave the United States?

Even in a temporary downturn, why in the world would foreigners ever want to pull out of their U.S. investments when the rest of the world will offer even worse returns?

Again, this is an excellent question, one that seems very reasonable, until you dig below the surface. On the face of it, it makes good sense to say that in a global downturn, foreign investors will still find better profits in the U.S. than any where else . . . except for one problem that could eat up all their potential U.S. profits: the risk of a falling dollar.

While the profits on U.S. stocks and bonds remain small, the increasing risk of potentially losing those small returns because of a falling dollar becomes quite large. For example, if you can get a 3 percent return on a German bond and 4 percent on a U.S. bond, it makes good sense to buy American. However, if the value of the dollar drops 5 percent, all of a sudden your 4 percent return on you U.S. bond instantly transforms into a 1 percent loss—which is far worse than making a 3 percent profit in Germany. And the risk of the dollar dropping 5 percent is increasingly more likely.

The same is true for the stock market. A 5 percent increase in the market can be completely wiped out by a 5 percent fall in the value of the dollar.

So the answer is yes, even in a downturn, investing in our stocks and bonds can yield returns as good as, if not better than, the rest of the world. But when you factor in the risk of a falling dollar, foreign investors are going to start finding our assets looking very unattractive indeed. The greater the perceived risk that the dollar may fall, the less foreign investors will be interested in U.S. assets over the long run.

But that is only one side of the push-pull equation. Not only will investors become increasingly pushed away from U.S. assets because of the falling dollar, they will also be pulled toward a giant, irresistible magnet: huge potential profits in gold and euros.

The more investors are attracted to gold and euros and repelled from the dollar and other U.S. assets, the faster they are going to want to sell what they don't want

(U.S. stocks, bonds, etc.) and buy what they do want (gold and euros). Many investors are already doing just that. And in time, many, many more will join them.

It all adds up to only one outcome: Sooner or later, the dollar is going down.

Won't foreign investors just rush back to buy cheaper U.S. assets when the dollar falls?

Under more normal conditions, that would make sense. In this situation, the answer is no, because there will have been a fundamental shift in the value of U.S. assets. Think about it like the stock market. If a company's stock falls quite low there is only one reason to rush in and buy it: you believe in its future potential growth because its fundamental value is there, based on rational economic factors. In the case of the United States, immediately after the dollar falls and the rest of the bubbles pop, there is not immediate reason to believe in fundamental value. Long-term, the U.S. certainly has the potential of coming back, but in the immediate future, following the pop, few investors will want to put their money where there is no fundamental value and won't be for quite a while.

Investors will be even less likely to come back immediately to the U.S. because they will be busy making money in other investments, like gold and euros.

Wait a minute! When Bubblequake hits the whole world, won't U.S. assets still be more profitable than other countries?

Yes, they will. But with the value of the dollar significantly falling, any profits that foreign investors might make on their U.S. assets will be diminished or lost when they convert their U.S. dollars into their own currencies. That will make U.S. assets look a lot less attractive.

Why Has the Federal Reserve Raised Interest Rates So Substantially?

The Federal Reserve has raised interest rates (the cost of borrowing money) more than 400 percent since 2004. The most common explanation for this would be to fight the threat of inflation. At least, that's what Fed Chairman Ben Bernanke would say.

But is this really the best way to fight inflation? Wouldn't it be better to simply decrease the money supply? Isn't that the fastest, most effective way to fight inflation? Raising interest rates is really not such an efficient way to handle inflation.

However, raising interest rates is a very good way to handle something else—attract even more foreign capital into the United States. If that is a priority, then raising interest rates is absolutely the best thing the Fed can do. And if the Chinese have been sending quiet signals that they are having trouble buying so many dollars to prop up the value of the dollar, then raising interest rates is the best thing you can do to help out your Chinese friends (of course, they are doing it to maintain their exports, not because they are our friends).

But you have to admit the Chinese have been awfully friendly to the dollar lately. As we've pointed out many times, massive dollar purchases by China, and formerly by Japan, have been essential to maintaining the dollar's value and, hence, the value of all the massive investments that foreigners have made in our stocks, government bonds and real estate. Without this massive support, the dollar will fall, and the price of those assets could crash dramatically.

So, you have to wonder, is it really inflation we are fighting with interest rate hikes or are we really fighting to maintain the dollar?

If we had to make one recommendation to the Federal Reserve to keep America's Bubble Economy from bursting, it would be this: Keep raising those interest rates as much as possible so we can keep the Chinese happy.

It's funny, that's exactly what the Fed is doing.

How can you possibly say the dollar will fall?

Most people think of the dollar as the best, most stable, and most rationally controlled currency the world has ever known. The dollar is so rock-solid here and around the globe that some people consider it the world's reserve currency, like gold used to be. Everyone wants dollars! How is it possible that someday the royal dollar may no longer be king?

As hard as it is for us to conceive, the mighty dollar is about to take a beating. Right now, China and Japan are heavily manipulating the dollar to prop up its value and maintain their exports. We might like to think of the dollar "as good as gold," but in reality our current dollar is nothing like the gold of the past. Today, no country needs a reserve of dollars. They can simply buy more dollars any time they wish with their own currency at a market price. In the past, foreign trade depended on gold. When a country ran out of gold, it couldn't trade anymore—except as straight barter. This was also an inherent protection from running a trade deficit. Going off the gold standard in 1973 for international trade opened a Pandora's box of troubles because it allowed us to have the huge trade imbalance (International Trade Deficit Bubble) we have today.

So buying dollars won't do anything to help a country like China build its reserves. It's just another commodity that can go up and down. And now, because it is being heavily manipulated to go up (creating the Dollar Bubble), the dollar is very vulnerable to going down. The Chinese would be better off buying gold if they wanted reserves, but that wouldn't suit their purpose of propping up the dollar to maintain their exports. The question is, how long will the Chinese be able to keep buying dollars to keep our Dollar Bubble afloat?

Even if the dollar does take a dip, we've always handled fluctuations before. Why will this time be any different?

This is another good question. It's very reasonable to say we've had ups and downs with the dollar before, and the U.S. Federal Reserve (our government's central bank) has always handled it just fine, so why worry?

There's no question that the dollar has been the most stable currency in the world and the Fed has been able to handle every temporary fluctuation. This time, however, will be very different for two reasons. First, the sheer number of dollars involved has become very, very large—far too large for the Federal Reserve to handle.

If foreigners owned $500 billion in U.S. assets, as they did in 1980, the Fed, with a little stress, could handle major movements of dollars, up to 20 percent or 30 percent. But now that foreign-owned U.S. assets are well over $10 trillion, even a 10 percent movement would be way beyond anything the Fed could handle, because now a 10 percent movement equals $1 trillion. And what if it's more than 10 percent? Huge amounts of currency can move out of this country in a heartbeat. The U.S. Federal Reserve is simply out of its league.

The other reason the Fed won't be able to save the dollar from a significant fall in value is that our government is no longer the only player involved. This time, we have the Japanese and Chinese heavily manipulating the dollar and because of that manipulation, the dollar is now potentially a very unstable currency, just like any stock or commodity that is heavily manipulated.

The U.S. and many other countries will certainly fight to the very end to prevent the dollar from falling. However, even big powerful countries do have their limits. The Chinese and the Japanese may have to stop buying dollars one day because, just like American consumers, they can't always buy everything they want to buy, even if they really, really want to buy it.

Governments cannot control everything, especially the psychology of investors in other countries or even the psychology of investors in their own countries. When investor psychology begins to sour, it will be impossible for central banks to buy all the dollars necessary to prevent a major fall. China and Japan are heavily buying dollars now because they feel there is little risk. Once it seems risky, their appetites may change. Even if China and Japan hang tough and keep buying dollars, other countries like Taiwan and South Korea may lose interest, recognizing that if they get out early, they won't suffer as big a loss. Whenever a bubble begins to fall, the last one out is a rotten egg. If they remain too long, China and Japan will find out just how truly rotten that can be.

Why all the fuss about the trade deficit? If we want to buy a whole lot more stuff from other countries than they buy from us, because we're rich and they are selling cheap, why shouldn't we?

Here's the problem with the current situation:

1. We buy lots of foreign goods. This moves billions (now almost a trillion) of our dollars out of the U.S. and into the hands of foreigners each year.

2. A flood of U.S. dollars in other countries makes the value of these dollars fall (big supply, lower demand and lower price). In fact, our dollar is now down 35 percent from its prior peak against the euro.

3. Foreigners use their U.S. dollars to buy U.S. assets, including our stocks, bonds, real estate, mortgages, etc. In a way, these are our exports.

4. Because foreigners already have lots of U.S. dollars (which we gave them for all the stuff we bought), private investors will only buy more U.S. dollars if they think the value of the dollar is rising. If they think the value is falling, they won't buy much.

5. The lack of private investors to buy dollars and the threat of a falling dollar, puts pressure on China and Japan to buy massive amounts of dollars to prop up the price (so we can keep buying their stuff). They will probably keep buying dollars for as long as they

can keep it up, but at some point, they will run out of money to buy dollars.

6. In the meantime, if the stock market continues to perform poorly (down 5 percent from mid 2000 to 2006 compared to the Japanese stock market up almost 50 percent in 2005), then foreign investors will eventually want to sell their U.S. stocks and bonds. This will push up interest rates and make the stock market decline.

7. High interest rates and a falling stock market will further slow the U.S. economy, pushing the value of the dollar even lower. Foreign capital will move out of the country in a flight to safety (and huge profits in gold and euros), and our bubbles will pop.

Borrowing from foreigners to fund U.S. government deficits has never been a problem before. Why is it a problem now?

For one thing, we never have borrowed from foreigners to this extent before. We never ran these kind of peacetime deficits and when we did run a wartime deficit in World War II, it was financed internally. So, we've never had to face the risk of a pullout of this much capital from the U.S. economy before.

With over $8 trillion (and rising) in debt to service, if interest rates hit 20 percent, the interest payments alone would consume almost *all* of our noncorporate federal income tax. And 20 percent interest rates are very possible if there is any significant withdrawal of foreign money from the U.S.

In the end, our government will simply have to print more money to pay down the interest on this astronomical debt, but that will just drive up inflation, making our dollars worth even less.

Our Total Government Debt May Be $8 Trillion, But It's Only Increasing by $300 Billion a Year, So We're Doing Fine, Right?

Many economists and financial analysts say our government deficit is manageable because it is less than 5 percent of our GNP. Of course, they are talking about our *annual* deficit. They aren't talking about our *cumulative* deficit which is now more than 60 percent of our GNP.

That's like a 500-pound man saying he's very healthy because he only gained 5 percent more fat this year. Even if he gained only 1 percent more fat, he's obviously in big trouble.

The key to our economic health is not merely what we are adding to our debt, but how much debt we already have accumulated. In economics, this difference is referred to as stock (cumulative amounts) versus flow (added amounts). What's happening now is we only want to talk about the flow and we are ignoring the stock.

Just as a 500-pound man is very vulnerable to health problems and considered "high risk" by his doctor, or as a consumer or corporation with large amounts of debt is very vulnerable to financial problems and is considered "high risk" by their lender, so too is a government at risk when it carries so much accumulated debt.

Yes, it's true, the government can always print more money to cure its debt ills, but wait until you see what happens when they turn on the presses (see Chapter 3).

The focus on the annual deficit, rather than the cumulative debt is an obvious oversight, clearly biased toward minimizing the problem. The real question is why do so many economists and financial analysts not point this out?

*What makes you think you know more than the experts?
If something big was about to happen, wouldn't the
experts be talking about it?*

Not necessarily. Often a very good sign of trouble can
be found, not in what people say, but in what they *don't* say.
What the experts aren't saying about all this speaks volumes.

Here's a good example. Nobody, and we really do
mean nobody, ever talks about the enormous positive economic benefits of running the nation with foreign-funded
government deficits. They never say one word about how
wonderful foreign-funded government debt has been for
creating new jobs and boosting the economy. How come?
Surely, if they wanted to, the experts could very easily
make the argument that foreign-funded government debt
has been one of the most important keys to our economic
growth since the early 1980s. Even if they don't think of it
as the most important driver of our economic boom, certainly it would make their list of the top ten reasons we are
where we are today. Yet nobody, anywhere, says much
about this.

Commentators do sometimes talk about the benefits
of running a big *trade deficit*, but not about the benefits of
running a big foreign-funded domestic government deficit.
Why?

Our best guess is simple: the experts don't publicly
discuss the economy-building power of foreign-funded
government deficits because they understand how delicate
the situation now is. If a big foreign-funded deficit is key to
expanding our economy and the stock market, then you
clearly have a bubble and a bubble can't last. Not only that,
you have a bubble whose future depends on the actions of

non-Americans, which makes us even more vulnerable. So, you don't talk about it and hope no one will bring it up.

But it is getting harder and harder to ignore the $8 trillion debt elephant in the middle of the room. Imagine how hard it's going to be to ignore when that elephant starts to stampede out the door. Sooner or later, economists will have to start talking about this. (And when they do, remember where you read about it first!)

Wait a minute! Isn't the United States the strongest, most successful nation the world has ever seen? Don't we have the most powerful currency, the most powerful army, the most powerful economy? Isn't that why they call us a Super Power? Let's get real! The United States is, was, and always will be economic king of the world!

It's interesting. We used to run into a lot more people with this kind of a reaction than we do today, particularly

"SORENSEN WILL PUT A POSITIVE SPIN ON IT, NISSEN WILL ISSUE A DENIAL, AND SIMS WILL FLAT OUT LIE ABOUT IT."

Source: cartoonstock.com

before the Internet Bubble popped. In the last few years, their numbers have faded considerably. Whether we officially know it or not, Americans are starting to feel "something" coming, particularly a downturn in real estate.

The fantasy that having a big army somehow makes our economy immune from foreign economic forces is ridiculous, but it's part of the denial that keeps us from facing facts. It also shows a bit of desperation on the part of investors who are running out of reasons to believe that there are no bubbles out there, especially the Dollar Bubble. Desperation is usually a sign that the end is near. When investor psychology turns, there will be no place for our bubbles to go but down.

Does it have to happen exactly the way you say it will happen?

No. The bursting of our bubble economy could potentially happen in many different ways. But given the current state of the dollar, the stock market, the real estate market, the degree of consumer and government debt, our huge trade deficits, and most of all, the presence of so much foreign capital in the United States that could quickly move out, it most definitely *will happen*. It's only a question of when.

Is there any chance investor psychology could improve, rather than sour?

If investors could just avoid ever getting nervous about their money, they would never pull it out of the stock market, our multiple bubbles would never collide and we could all live happily ever after. But if past behavior is a guide, don't count on it. Just like when the Internet Bubble popped, sooner or later, investors and their advisors will find it increasingly difficult to maintain confidence in stocks that continue to decline. It's reasonable to assume that savvy investors will eventually react rationally to over-priced stocks and overvalued dollars.

Won't the government solve this problem before it turns into a crisis?

Not likely. Even if they saw it coming, few politicians would be willing to purposely devalue the dollar or deflate the stock market. Governments—like the people they represent—often resist change until they have no choice. And no one resists change more than those who benefit most from the status quo.

Instead, the government will just keep borrowing more and more money. Eventually, when they can borrow no more, they will print more money. Of course, that will just get us into more trouble, by adding sky-high inflation to the rest of our woes.

Any chance we can just stall this thing in an endless waiting game?

Certainly, the government will try to do just that. But investors won't tolerate "waiting for Godot" forever. If they don't see a big upside potential, they won't tolerate a big downside risk for very much longer. Instead, they will move their investments to where there is less downside risk. As the downside risk becomes even clearer, they will move their money even faster. This is particularly true for the big insurance companies and other conservative investors in

Europe and Japan who have put a lot of money into the United States. Once the tide turns, there'll be nothing our government can do to stop the crash.

Okay, let's just say you might be right. How bad will things get?

For most people, pretty bad. Fortunately, the United States won't suffer as much as it did after the 1929 crash. And we won't be hit as hard as the rest of the world because our wealthy economy is far less dependent on exports than other nations. But we will certainly have a very different economy than we do today. Inflation and interest rates will soar, the dollar will buy far less than before, and many Americans will be mighty grumpy about it for a long, long time. (For more information on what life will be like after the bubbles pop, see **www.americasbubbleeconomy.com/howbadcanitget**.)

Alright already! You have my attention! How can I protect my assets and maybe even make some money on this thing?

The answer to this one is easy. Read the next chapter!

Won't This Just Be Our Children's Problem?

Often, when discussing the long-term problems of the government deficit, financial analysts, economists, and commentators say we are creating a massive problem for our children or our grandchildren. Almost no one says we are creating a massive problem for ourselves. Is that really true?

If the government deficit were the only bubble out there, we might be able to postpone the day of reckoning for some time, although probably not until our children's time. However, the government deficit is not a bubble in isolation, but is tied to all the other bubbles. If any one bubble starts to pop, the big government deficit bubble will be close behind. And, it won't wait until our children grow up. The government deficit bubble will pop as soon as the United States has trouble attracting foreign investment to fund its deficit. Like any heavily indebted individual or company, we're in great shape as long as the bank keeps lending us money. The day that stops, we are all in deep trouble, no matter how old our children are.

This is just one more example of how important it is to look at all the bubbles in the economy and not just one. It's not only smart, it is the way the economy really works—as a whole—everything included.

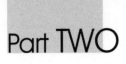

Part TWO

Profit When It Pops
with Alternative Investments

Chapter FIVE

Cashing in on Chaos

How to Cover Your Assets and Make Big Profits with Alternative Investments When the Bubbles Burst

Finally! We've arrived at that wonderful silver lining we keep telling you about. Actually, there's so much money to be made on this temporary black cloud that the silver lining will be truly golden.

Those of us who are willing to face facts early and move quickly and correctly, will not only be able to cover our assets while others lose their shirts (and pants and shoes . . .), we can even make huge profits on this unusual moment in history, perhaps more money than you ever thought possible.

That's because, unlike in the past, this particular set of bubbles has something few past bubbles could ever hope to provide: A real chance to profit, not only as the bubbles go up, but also as the bubbles come down.

How is that possible? If we make money on a bubble by buying when prices are low and selling when prices are high, how in the world are we going to make a profit when prices fall? Isn't the best we can hope for is not to take too big a loss?

Under normal conditions, all that is true. But as you probably have noticed by now, these are not exactly normal conditions. The big difference with this set of unique circumstances is that we do not have a single, isolated bubble (like the Dutch Tulip Bubble) where the price of one particular item (for example, tulip bulbs) has temporarily gone sky high and then crashes back to earth. No, in this particular golden moment, we have *multiple bubbles*—some rising and many falling. So, instead of just saving your neck by getting out of a bubble before it falls, this time you can hop off one bubble as it falls and onto another bubble as it rises.

And here's the really good news: you don't have to be rich to get a whole lot richer. The Dutch tulip investors would be spring-green with envy.

A Massive Transfer of Wealth

As terrible as our temporary cloud will be for the United States and other nations, the bursting of America's Bubble Economy will also be a real godsend for many smart, reasonable people who figure out how to be on the receiving end of what will be a truly massive transfer of wealth.

By "transfer of wealth," we mean the movement of wealth from some individuals and businesses to other individuals and businesses. Whether wealth transfers *away* from you or *towards* you, during this very unusual window of opportunity, is largely in your own hands—literally. Right now you are holding the *introductory* information you need to move fast, cover your assets, and create significant wealth when the bubble economy falls. Think of this chapter as "Transfer of Wealth 101"—not every detail each individual may need to know, but a basic foundation for thinking differently about your assets and investments and a starting point for learning more about how to apply this new way of thinking to your own unique financial situation.

We all know the age-old expression "the rich get richer." History has certainly proven it to be true. Now, however, we are about to enter a rare period in which not only the rich but also the so-called "little guy" has a real opportunity to cash in big—if we play it smart. And frankly, we better play it smart because those of us who are not currently among the super wealthy have a particularly pressing need to protect our limited assets and make each and every investment work.

The coming months and years will offer all sorts of highly unusual financial opportunities at a time when we also have a great deal of handy financial tools that were not previously available. "Shorting" the market, for example, has been around for years, but now we can also "short" currency and bond futures. We now have a more sophisticated market for trading stock options. And beyond stocks, there is a bonanza to be made by buying and leveraging gold and euros (discussed in the following pages). With electronic trading just a few mouse clicks away, access to United States and world markets has never been easier or faster, with or without a broker.

A Word About Risk

Naturally, all these golden opportunities also carry some risks. *Risk* is traditionally a four letter word when it comes to investing, and certainly, the less of it, the better. But the risks you may face by taking steps to protect current assets and create significant future wealth during the coming Bubble-quake are relatively minor compared to the truly terrible, *100 percent guaranteed risk* of sitting back and doing nothing while one's assets evaporate right before your eyes and once-in-a-lifetime opportunities permanently pass you by.

Later in the chapter, we discuss ways you can assess your own level of risk tolerance to help guide you in your personal decision-making process. For now, please understand this: There are many, many times in life when doing nothing is absolutely the smartest, safest, best thing to do. This, dear reader, is not one of them.

Of course, each individual's specific financial situation is unique and we always recommend that you consult your professional financial and tax advisors before selling or buying any assets. The authors and their expert associates are available for customized consulting to individuals and business, based on the ideas and analysis introduced in the book. What follows, however, is a general discussion of our general views on general asset protection and general wealth creation during the coming general economic changes. Get the general idea?

Customized Analysis for Your Specific Industry, Business, or Investment Goals

The authors and their economic experts and experienced business valuators can apply rigorous economic analysis to a variety of industries and businesses, based on the ideas introduced in this book. Individual investors, investment bankers and other investment professionals can also benefit from personalized consulting to suit their particular needs.

Country-specific analysis can be customized for rapidly changing conditions in the United States, Europe, Asia, or the Middle East.

For more information, please contact The Foresight Group at 800–994–0018.

Above All Else, Cover Thy Assets

Let's start with the basics: survival.

There are five nonnegotiable bedrock commandments for covering one's assets and eliminating (or at least, minimizing) one's losses during the difficult times ahead. Most of these rules have to do with what you should not do in the run up to the coming multiple bubble collapse. No doubt, some of these rules will seem contrary to your current investment thinking and may require some serious thought before you are willing to act.

Asset-Covering Commandment 1: Thou Shall Avoid All Real Estate Purchases Except for Personal Use

In general, real estate is overvalued and on the way down. Although there may be some growth potential left in some isolated real estate markets, the next two to six years are certainly not the right time to add to your real estate portfolio. Even if some markets rebound after a dip, any recovery will likely be short-lived, and the potential risks of investing in real estate over the next several years far outweigh the possible benefits.

We understand that this rule may feel as uncomfortable as sleeping in a tent. Buying investment real estate has traditionally been a reliable foundation for building future wealth. But we have to face facts. American real estate is in a bubble. Long-term, the only direction the housing bubble is going to move is south, probably even into the deep south.

Although it may not be right around the corner, we are simply too close to the bubble collapse to see any significant upside in real estate. It is far more likely that you will suffer a loss, perhaps even a massive loss if you don't get out early enough. Now is a good time to sell any investment real estate that you own other than your home (you have to live someplace). By selling now, you may get less than you would like; but it is too hard to time the market perfectly to make holding it worthwhile. Besides, as you will see later in this chapter, there are much better places to put your money.

As tempting as it may be, we suggest that you do not hold onto rental income property. When the bubbles pop, your rental income will not compensate you for the loss of equity when the value of your real estate, in inflation adjusted terms, plummets. You would be much better off simply selling all your investment real estate before the bubbles crash and putting that money in much higher-return investments, which are explained later. As mentioned earlier, each individual situation is unique and we are not suggesting that we know what is in your particular best interest. It is important to consult a tax advisor before selling any real estate, particularly if you anticipate a capital gain.

Asset-Covering Commandment 2: Thou Shall Avoid Most Stocks Like the Plague

There are three vital reasons for avoiding stocks:

- The stock market is up tenfold in 20 years without an equal rise in real earnings, therefore we have a bubble.

- The stock market has been performing poorly for the last five years, therefore it's only a matter of time before investor confidence wanes.

- When foreign investors buy fewer U.S. stocks, they also buy fewer U.S. bonds. When they buy fewer U.S. bonds, interest rates climb and stock values fall.

Bottom line: Most stocks are overvalued and on their way down.

Will there be some ups and downs? Of course. Is it worth taking a chance on it? We think not. As with real estate, although there may be some potential growth left in the stock market, the timing is very tricky and it's not worth taking the risk. In the short run, you are about as likely to lose as to gain. And in the long run, all you will do is lose significantly when stock values begin to seriously plummet. Again, we will show you much better places to put your money.

We know the idea of getting out of the market may be unappealing, especially if you've been in a while and you've made some money. Remember, be smart, be reasonable. The Dow is up tenfold in 20 years. Real earnings in this same time period are not. The last five years have been pretty lackluster for the U.S. stock market. It's time to get out and position yourself for much bigger returns elsewhere.

An exception to this general rule is individual stocks. There will certainly continue to be individual stocks that do quite well before the bubbles burst. If you can pick them, more power to you. Just keep your eyes open and be ready to unload fast on a moment's notice.

Another exception: If you hold stock options in a company whose value may grow rapidly, you may want to keep them since there is no downside risk to holding an option. More than one of the authors currently holds stock options in companies that may do very well over the next year or two. However, it never hurts to lock in a profit on some of your holdings. Don't wait too long to liquidate; eventually economic gravity is going to kick in and our bubbles—most likely starting with the Stock Market Bubble—will fall.

Foreign Investors Don't Love Us, They Love the Money We Make Them

The simple, yet important truth is that foreign investors will only love us as long as we make them money. If the dollar falls precipitously and they start losing money in the United States, they will take their money and run. If the stock market also falls (and it will), they will run even faster. Sometimes people mistakenly think foreigners invest in the United States because they are so impressed with us. Remember, it's not about us, it's about profits. And that, unfortunately, can change on a dime.

Asset-Covering Commandment 3: Thou Shall Avoid Long-Term Bonds and Bond Funds

Interest rates will rise prior to the bubbles falling and will certainly rise very dramatically after the fall. Hence, there's little reason to invest in long-term bonds or bond funds now. The premium for long-term is far too minimal to be worth the risk. You can probably push it for another year or two, but for the small extra return, is it really worth it?

Asset-Covering Commandment 4: Thou Shall Avoid All Evil Adjustable-Rate Debt

All adjustable-rate loans, credit cards, and adjustable or variable mortgages will become an absolute disaster when the bubbles burst. Interest rates will rise dramatically and so will your mortgage and other payments if you don't get out of these soon. Now is a great time to lock in low long-term interest rates. Don't take chances; get rid of your evil variable-rate mortgage and other big debts now!

On the other hand, assuming your credit card debt is not that significant, there is no great urgency to pay it off immediately. Even low-balance adjustable-rate cards can be held a bit longer. But do unload these before the Bubblequake because interest rates are going to skyrocket and credit terms on your cards will not be pretty.

If you have investment or personal-use real estate currently financed at a variable rate, unload these now, either by selling the real estate or refinancing the loan. If you don't, you will be sunk when the bubbles burst and your rate shoots way up. Please get out now, while the getting is good.

Asset-Covering Commandment 5: Thou Shall Not Depend on Fixed Payment Pensions

High interest rates and high inflation, coupled with collapsing asset values and a slew of corporate bankruptcies will make any fixed payment plan a complete loser. Many plans have some inflation protection built into the contract, but it likely won't be enough to compensate for very high rates of inflation. Also, even if the contract requires it, the plan may not be able to provide all the protection it promises. Even now, during the best of economic times, many pension plans, including many state and local government pension plans, are seriously underfunded. Clearly, during the coming bubble meltdown, this will only get much worse.

Even funds covered by the Pension Benefit Guaranty Corporation (PBGC) are at real risk once our bubble troubles get rolling because the PBGC could easily become overwhelmed. And funds not covered by the PBGC will be in even worse shape because they probably won't be bailed out by the government, which will struggle mightily to deal with its own massive debt and massive interest costs.

Beyond Survival: Cashing in on the Coming Bubblequake

Covering one's assets is absolutely essential and should not be put off for too long. Once this step is taken care of, you (and your assets) will be free to move onto the really exciting part of the coming Bubblequake. Unlike any other bubble crash, in which all you can hope for is to not take too big a loss, this bubble crash provides something truly unique: the opportunity to jump off one set of falling bubbles to catch a ride up on some other rising bubbles.

Taking advantage of the many money-making opportunities ahead will require an open mind, some liquid assets, and the willingness to look into three potential treasure chests full of tools for milking this Bubblequake for all its worth. Below is an overview of each of these big profit opportunities, followed by a more detailed discussion of how you can customize your approach to suit your own particular financial situation and personal degree of risk tolerance.

As a reminder, please note that we have already

warned you to avoid most stocks and real estate like the plague. These are the two areas where most of your friends and colleagues are going to take the biggest initial hit. People may not necessarily understand why you are getting out of stocks and real estate in the next couple of years. Don't let your investment decisions become a popularity contest; make your own well-reasoned decisions. After the bubbles pop, you are going to look like a genius.

Can Financial Panic Be Rational?

Most definitely *yes*.

When asset values are rapidly dropping and there is little fundamental value to justify hanging on, then selling as quickly as possible makes the most rational sense. Panic only becomes irrational when you sell assets for less than their fundamental value, and then someone else comes along and buys up your bargain, eventually reselling it at a higher price. Irrational panic sets in when emotions overtake sound financial decision making.

Many times, however, panic is the best, most rational response. When Internet stocks began to fail, selling quickly was the smartest, most rational thing to do. Sure, you could have done even better if you could time every little up and down before the crash, but even without perfect timing, you would have done quite well if you simply panicked and sold everything when the Internet Bubble popped in March 2000.

We call this "Rational Panic," and it is exactly what will happen when stocks and dollars begin to fall in the Bubblequake. It will be extremely difficult to time every up and down with enough precision to not get hurt, and doing nothing will only increase your losses on the way to a very big, very steep drop ahead. Instead of trying to shoot

143

the rapids on your way to a dangerous waterfall, your most logical move is Rational Panic—paddle frantically to shore, sell as quickly as possible, and get out before you drown.

Alternative Investments in Gold—Opening the Gold Treasure Chest

Let's get something clear right up front: We are not gold bugs. Like most smart, reasonable people, we don't jump on (or off) bandwagons based on wishful thinking or a habit of seeing only doom and gloom. Traditionally, the warning to "buy gold" has been the longtime mantra of the chronically pessimistic. More recently, however, an entirely new, much more optimistic crowd is starting to buy gold, too, and for

"We were wondering if __now__ would be a good time to panic?"

very good reason. Prior to and during the coming collapse of America's Bubble Economy, there are several very compelling arguments for investing in gold (see "Gold Bugs" sidebar).

We won't bore you with more details than you really need to know. As other asset values decline, people want to put their money somewhere. They want to buy something, preferably something of rising value that has a long tradition of acceptance and demand during difficult times. That is gold. As demands continues to rise for gold, and then rapidly rises when the other bubbles pop, the price of gold will shoot up. As the price of gold shoots up, gold buying is converted to speculative bubble buying, insuring a vast rise due to the typical conditions that propel a bubble forward. The rising gold bubble is your very best bet for profits during the coming Bubblequake.

Will the Gold Bubble fall back down? Of course it will; it's a bubble, isn't it? But why not go for the ride? This could be one of the longest rides of any bubble—10 to 20 years. Compared to other assets, such as stocks and bonds, the amount of gold now available is relatively tiny (see Figure 5.1). You can count on more gold being mined in the future to satisfy growing demand, but demand will surely outpace supply, pushing up the price.

Huge and growing demand; relatively tiny supply—you do the math.

The "Gold Bugs" Are Right . . . Sort of

The gold bugs are right. Gold will be a spectacular investment after the bubbles pop and a very good investment before they pop.

Figure 5.1 Value of World Stock Market versus Value of World Investment Gold Market

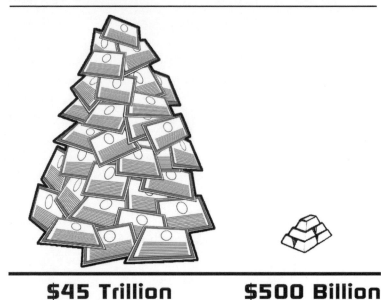

$45 Trillion $500 Billion

In relation to world stock markets, the world gold market is truly tiny. That means a relatively small movement of capital out of stocks and into gold will drive up gold prices massively.

On the other hand, the gold bugs are wrong. The reasons that gold will be a spectacular investment has nothing to do with some fundamental quality of gold itself, but will primarily result from the other bubbles colliding and popping, and investor interest rationally shifting to gold—for a while. Eventually, gold values will collapse (as bubbles always do), making the Gold Bubble the biggest, baddest financial bubble of the 21st century.

All that will be many years away. In the meantime, as the Gold Bubble goes up, here are the top 12 *rational reasons* to join the gold rush:

1. The gold market is very, very small compared to the stock and bond markets. Even a small shift of capital out of these markets and into gold will greatly boost the gold market. Any large inflow of capital into gold will have a very huge positive effect, indeed (see Figure 5.1).

2. Gold is easily sold for euros, giving investors a double benefit. That means if you buy gold, you are indirectly buying euros at the same time, which is great because euros will also go when our bubble economy falls. If gold goes up four times, and the euro goes up two times against the dollar, your net increase is $4 \times 2 = 8$ times. Not bad at all.

3. Gold has significant potential for being an illegal tax avoidance technique. Once the bubbles collide, tax rates in the United States and around the world will increase and incomes will decline. The combination means that interest in tax avoidance, even if illegal, will skyrocket. Holding physical gold is a very effective way to avoid taxes in the United States and around the world. We, of course, do not advocate illegal tax avoidance, but there's no denying others will find this appealing, further boosting the demand for and the price of gold.

4. The gold market is much more of a world market than U.S. stocks and bonds. Foreigners can buy U.S. stocks and bonds, but buying gold is easier. Hence, gold has a much greater world demand. For example, currently, India is the world's biggest consumer of gold, buying 20 percent of the world's gold, about twice as much as U.S. investors. On the other hand, India is not a large consumer of U.S. stocks and bonds. Therefore, the ease in which worldwide investors can buy gold will also

heighten its appeal. Plus, gold already is a favorite for many investors in the Middle East and Asia.

5. It is very difficult to rapidly increase gold production. Gold mining will not be able to keep pace with demand for many years. When demand for gold goes up, so will the price.

6. Gold's value increases with inflation. Inflation will be very high in the United States and also in major European and Asian nations.

7. All the world's stock and bond markets will be under pressure. Investors will view gold as an excellent alternative.

8. If the banking system comes under severe stress, as it likely will, gold will have even further appeal.

9. Short term, the central banks of the world, which have been selling about 500 tons of gold a year since the 1999 Central Bank Gold Agreement, will likely reduce their sales. In fact, some central banks are already saying they will increase their gold reserves—in some cases, instead of buying dollars. 500 tons per year is no small issue given that South Africa, the world's largest gold producer, only produces about 300 tons a year. If central banks significantly reduce gold sales, supply will drop and prices will increase.

10. Short term, South Africa's production fell 15 percent in 2005. It isn't clear if declines will continue at this rate, but clearly, South African production will not increase any time soon. Again, lower supply and growing demand equal higher prices.

11. As bubble fever takes over, gold will become a shining investment star in an otherwise very grim investment landscape.

Timing the Coming Gold Bubble

Some people think we already have a gold bubble, that gold prices have reached their peak and are due for a fall. While the volatile gold market will continue to go up and down, the overall trend is most definitely still up—way up once the dollar falls and the rest of the bubbles pop.

Think of gold as having two stages of growth over the next several years: the first, relatively small but profitable, and the second very large and very profitable. Although we view gold as a long-term investment—meaning the real upside won't start for another two to five years or more—there will likely continue to be good appreciation in gold in the meantime. Gold has already doubled in value since 2001 in a fairly consistent bull market and could easily double again in the next five years. While this increase pales in comparison to the coming growth in gold, doubling in five years is really quite good, certainly better than current stock market returns. By nature, gold always is somewhat volatile; but long-term, we see very little downside risk.

Of course, the rapidly rising value of gold, now and in the future, is itself another bubble—only this one is on its way *up*. Hopping off a falling bubble and onto a rising bubble will be your key to making huge profits while others take a beating. This is where that huge "transfer of wealth" we talked about earlier comes into play. Gold is and will continue to be a rising bubble. Don't watch from the sidelines; ride it up! (For more insight into why gold is an especially good bet right now, see Chapter 6, "Gold for People Who Hate Gold," by financial bubble expert Eric Janszen.)

Eventually, many years from now, after the worst

impact of the other bursting bubbles are felt, and after the credit and capital markets stabilize and begin to rebuild, the big fat Gold Bubble will rise no more and like all bubbles fall back to earth.

In the meantime, here are your four wealth-building power tools from the gold treasure chest.

Gold Power Tool 1: Buy Gold Bullion Bars and Coins

The most fun—but somewhat more expensive—way to buy gold is to buy actual bullion bars or bullion coins such as the American Eagle or the South African Krugerrand. Coins are one ounce (but are also struck in smaller one-half ounce and one-tenth ounce amounts) and are often a bit more expensive than bars, which come in 1 ounce and 10 ounce. You can buy these from local coin shops, where they are a bit more expensive per ounce than buying online. However, there are no postage, shipping, or insurance charges. Some states may charge sales tax or, like Maryland, may require that you buy at least $1,000 worth of gold in order to be tax exempt. The best way to find a local coin shop is to check your local yellow pages.

Buying bullion online or by phone may be the best way to buy bullion for many people. Simply type "gold bullion" into the search bar of your favorite Internet search engine and start investigating your options. We've had good luck with a few good vendors. Please visit our web site at **www .americas bubbleeconomy.com/buygold** for links to gold vendors.

One problem with buying gold bullion is storage. You can keep it at home, but for extra security, you might want to store it in a safe deposit box. Even a small box can hold quite a lot of gold. Another problem comes when you want to sell your gold and you have to return to the store for a "buy" price that is less than the "sell" price.

Gold Power Tool 2: Buy Gold from a Gold Depository

In addition to storage problems and the hassles and cost of buying and selling physical gold, the bigger issue with buying physical gold is you miss out on the considerable advantages of buying gold on margin. For leveraging gold and for ease of ownership of physical gold, we recommend looking at depositories. For our recommendations, please visit our web site at **www.americasbubbleeconomy.com/buygold** for links to gold depositories.

Buying gold from a depository means you always keep direct legal ownership of the gold, although not necessarily physical possession. If the depository went bankrupt (unlikely), the gold would still be yours. As soon as you buy it, they sign legal ownership over to you and deposit it with a separate legal entity. Also, at any time, you can ask for your physical gold to be shipped to you.

Some depositories allow you to buy gold on margin, putting 30 percent down and obtaining the rest on credit. That means you can use, say $3,000, to buy up to $10,000 worth of gold, or $30,000 to buy $100,000 worth of gold. Like buying anything on margin, you have to be careful. If the price of gold falls, you will have to make up the difference in equity, plus pay some other fees. Even in an overall bull market, there can be short-lived reversals. If you overleverage, you can be caught in a downdraft in the market.

Still, buying physical gold at a reasonable margin can be a great way to grab a ticket to ride on the rising Gold Bubble.

Gold Power Tool 3: Buy Gold ETFS

Gold ETFs (Exchange Traded Funds) first came on the scene in the fall of 2005 and are now traded like stock on the New York Stock Exchange under the symbols GLD and IAU. The price of one share of a gold ETF is set at one-tenth the price of an ounce of gold. When gold goes up, gold ETFs go up, too. The advantage is that you needn't buy large quantities of gold to get in on the gold action. Unlike stocks, each ETF share is backed by physical gold. You can even have the physical gold shipped to you if you like.

You can read more about specific ways to buys gold ETFs through links on our web site at **www.americasbubble economy.com/buygold.**

Gold ETFs account for more than 300 tons of gold bought by investors as of early 2006. Currently, there are only about 3,500 tons of gold sold each year, worldwide, for all purposes (including jewelry, industrial, and investment), so that is a very impressive amount of gold (almost 10 percent) after only six months in existence.

Also of interest for some investors, a silver ETF and a combined silver/gold ETF are now also available.

Like physical gold, gold ETFs can also be bought on margin.

Don't Buy Stock in Gold Mining Companies

Many investors would rather buy stock than gold, so why not buy stock in companies that mine gold? Over the past few years, gold mining stocks have generally performed better than gold itself. However, we do not recommend gold stocks. Although they may continue to out-earn gold for the next couple of years, gold will do far better than gold stocks in the long run, and when the stock market declines, it will take gold mining stocks with it.

If you wish to invest in gold stocks to try to catch some better returns than gold itself over the next couple of years, we recommend you buy a *gold stock fund* rather than individual gold stocks, which tend to be somewhat more volatile. As with all stock, you can make money by picking the right company at the right time, but you have to be very careful.

Now, let's look into your second treasure chest of wealth-building power tools.

The Gold Bubble: The Biggest, Baddest Bubble of Them All

Although gold performs spectacularly after the other bubbles pop, it is important to recognize that, like the stock market and the dollar, gold too will follow a classic up-down bubble trajectory. The coming Gold Bubble could easily last 10 or more years, and at its height, gold prices could become truly stratospheric—so high, in fact, we won't even mention our best guess for fear of losing credibility. (Of course, as soon as the Bubblequake hits, we will certainly tell you all about it.)

The reasons that the Gold Bubble will go up (see the sidebar Why the Gold Bugs Are Right—Sort Of) are actually the same reasons the Gold Bubble will go down only in reverse. Gold will go up when the other bubbles (stock, dollar, real estate) go down because investors will want to buy something seemingly stable and profitable while their other assets look increasingly unstable and unprofitable.

In time, however, the instability of other assets will evolve to stability again, and their huge downside risks will transform back to normal upside gains. In other words, it will make sense to buy them again. When that happens, the big fat Gold Bubble (like all bubbles) will dramatically fall.

Some people say there may be a fundamental shift away from intangible assets, such as stocks and bonds, whose value can easily evaporate depending on investor interest and government irresponsibility, and towards more tangible assets, like gold. This will be true for a while, perhaps even for quite a while—but not forever.

How far gold will fall depends on a couple of factors. It won't collapse completely because there is some commercial value for jewelry and industrial uses. However, for some period after the Gold Bubble pops, there will be a huge oversupply of gold, relative to industrial and jewelry demand. That will certainly push the price into the ground. With a huge oversupply and no investment demand, the price of gold will fall well below the cost of production, probably in the range of $50 per ounce when adjusted for inflation.

At some point, many years from now, private investors and central banks will no longer hold gold, and we will have finally completed our long evolution away from metal-based money to the next stage of money, as we explain in Chapter 8.

In the meantime, we highly suggest you join us on the wonderful ride up on the big fat Gold Bubble. You won't believe how high we're going.

**"Gold is finally making a move and
you sit here doing nothing."**

Alternative Investments in Euros—
Opening the Euro Treasure Chest

As the Dollar Bubble falls, the price of the euro will rise dramatically. Euros won't have the same appreciation potential as gold, but they will do very well during the coming Bubblequake.

Have your doubts? Well, Warren Buffet, America's greatest living investor, who has already invested heavily in euros, can't be wrong, can he? Well, of course, he can be wrong—in the short term. But, in the long-term, Buffet and some other big-time investors are showing some very good foresight. The value of the euro will continue to fluctuate against the dollar; but when the bough breaks and the dollar finally does fall, up go euros at least for a while.

Timing the Euro Bubble

Although it will be a bubble, because it will rise and fall, the euro bubble won't be nearly as dramatic as the gold bubble. To some degree, the rise in value of the euro relative to the dollar is a long-term adjustment to an overvalued dollar.

Timing on the euro will be trickier than gold. It hasn't shown the same solid bull market growth that gold has shown. However, the huge imbalance in foreign trade will put continuing pressure on the dollar. The U.S. Federal Reserve has and will continue to offset that by raising interest rates dramatically. But we can only raise rates for so long without damaging the economy a lot. As we have said, gold and euros are long-term investments, so now is about as good a time as any to buy. The Euro Bubble is a relatively weak bubble compared to recent bubbles. It will also be relatively short-lived, rising against the dollar until long-term exports and import equilibrate for the industrial world. It's hard to time it perfectly, as even the best of the best, Warren Buffet, has shown.

In addition to euros, the Japanese yen may also do well, relative to the dollar. However, the euro is much more widely traded, so we are focusing our discussion there.

There are two ways to invest in euros:

Euro Power Tool 1: Buy Euro ETFs

This is by far the easiest way to invest in euros. It is much easier than trying to play the currency futures markets, which we don't recommend for people who aren't skilled commodities traders. Euro ETFs were introduced to the market in December 2005. Like gold ETFs, these trade like stocks on the New York Stock Exchange. Its price is set at 100 times the price of a euro in dollars. So, if the price of the euro in dollars is $1.20, each euro ETF "share" sells for $120. When the value of the dollar falls, the value of the euro (in dollar terms) goes up, as does the "share" price of the euro ETF. The big downside of owning euro ETFs is there is no interest paid. The big upside is that euro ETFs can also be bought on margin.

You can find out more about how to buy euro ETFs on our web site at **www.americasbubbleeconomy.com/buyeuros.**

Euro Power Tool 2: Buy Physical Euros

You can also buy physical euros from your bank and hold them in a safe deposit box, like gold. This may have some attraction if you only want to hold a small amount or just want to see what a euro looks like, but the best way to invest in a lot of euros is through euro ETFs.

Again, the big downside of owning physical euros is there is no interest paid.

Euro Power Tool 3: Buy Short-Term Euro-Denominated Government Bonds

To overcome the problem of not receiving any interest on your euro ETFs or physical euros, you could alternatively invest in euro-denominated government bonds. Don't invest in euro-denominated corporate bonds because there is a risk of loss due to bankruptcy. Stick to government bonds.

Short-term euro-denominated government bonds or notes are most easily and most safely purchased through euro government bond mutual funds. For suggestions of good places to purchase these euro bond funds, please go to **www.americasbubbleeconomy.com/buyeuros**.

Alternative Investments in Emerging Markets

Emerging Markets—Foreign Stocks

There has been a great deal of interest in foreign stocks lately, due to their good performance. In fact, almost all foreign markets, except Chile's did better than the U.S. stock markets in 2005, in many cases twice as good as the United States. Japan's stock market performed more than five times as well as the U.S. market, rising more than 50 percent in 2005.

The correction of late spring 2006 put a damper on some of the enthusiasm for these emerging markets, but clearly significant interest remains and significant amounts of money are held in emerging markets. Short term, there may still be some money to be made in foreign stocks, but as in the U.S. stock market, you are playing a risky game. Plenty has been written on how best to invest in foreign markets, which we will not repeat here. From our point of view, as the bubbles start to pop, foreign markets are not good places to put your money. Unlike the euro, which will go up dramatically as the dollar falls, European and Asian stocks will fall dramatically, along with every other stock market around the world during the Bubblequake.

When the Bubbles pop, the old adage will remain true

with a vengeance: When America catches a cold, the world gets pneumonia.

Emerging Markets—Real Estate

Although interest in emerging markets has focused primarily on foreign stock markets, foreign real estate is also worth a brief mention. Real estate in some places such as India and China is currently experiencing a boom due to enormous growth in their economies. As incomes rise, a growing number of people will seek more expensive housing, driving up the price of existing housing and boosting home building. As we have seen in the U.S., a housing boom creates many new jobs, further stimulating the economy.

However, as we have said, when the bubbles pop, China and India will trade in their booming economies for a deep recession. Hence, like their stock markets, and perhaps even more so, real estate values in these countries will dramatically decline. Although there may be some money to be made from the boom before the bubbles burst, timing will be tricky. Therefore, in general, we find foreign real estate an emerging market to avoid from now on.

Bubblequake Around the World

Once the Bubblequake hits, it will be felt around the world because so many countries have been deeply involved in helping to create and maintain the bubbles in the United States.

The world is also very dependent upon the U.S. economy to drive much of the recent growth in other

---

countries. Where would China be without their enormous exports to the U.S.? Exports from Japan, Canada and Europe to the U.S. are also very important for maintaining those economies. As has often been said, we are the economic engine of growth for the world. When that engine stalls, the world will not be happy.

Those most dependent upon exports to the United States will feel the most pain, China and Japan being two very obvious examples. But Canada and Mexico will also suffer. Like in other economic disruptions, there may be some benefits, as well. In the case of China, the economic shock may be severe enough to create the final large-scale civilian unrest necessary to push China towards democracy.

Of course, the enormous losses sustained by foreign investors in the United States will add to the significant woes they will face back in their home countries. Japan and Europe, who have invested the most in the U.S., will suffer the greatest losses. In addition to private investors, governments that supported the dollar—China and Japan topping the list—will also be hit hard.

The less industrialized economies will feel the pain, as well. Worldwide prices for all major commodities, including oil, will fall, putting enormous pressure on Saudi Arabia and the other middle eastern oil exporters, which will further destabilize an already unstable region. South America and Africa, heavily dependent upon their commodities exports, will also suffer.

The United States may be most at fault due to its heavy borrowing and other economic mismanagement, but when a creditor as big as the U.S. has problems, it's not just the creditor's problem, it's also the bank's problem and all the creditor's suppliers.

Alternative Investments in Commodities

Commodities In General

In general, commodities traditionally go down in value when the economy goes down. However, this particular downturn will be different because of the dramatic fall in the dollar. The low value dollar makes U.S.-produced commodities low priced in foreign currencies. Even if demand is low in the rest of the world because of the Bubblequake, U.S.-produced commodities will often be much lower cost than those produced by other countries because of the low value of the dollar. So expect dollar prices for U.S.-produced goods such as oil, natural gas, coal, lumber, grain, beef, copper, and the like to be very good.

For a while our exports of such goods will increase, but dampened by the fact that the world is in a deep recession. Exactly how the twin forces of a cheap dollar and a worldwide recession will affect exports of U.S. produced commodities is a complex issues. One thing is certain though, dollar prices of U.S. produced commodities will be high. Equally certain is that the world prices in non-dollar terms will be quite low due to the worldwide drop in demand due to the worldwide recession.

For investors, these twin forces will produce a great deal of volatility. Increasingly, a commodities play will become a dollar play. Hence, because of this, the overall trend will be bullish, but this will be a very tricky area. Commodities are always volatile and the popping of the bubbles and impact of the falling dollar will make them even more volatile. This will not be a market for the feint of heart. Commodities trading in the Bubblequake will be like going from canoeing in a Class I rapid to shooting a Class V.

**As the Bubbles Pop, Gold Will Not Be Treated as a Commodity,
It Will Be in a Class by Itself**

Below we describe the specific impacts of the popping of
the bubbles on specific classes of commodities. But, first,
we want to point out that, as the bubbles pop, gold will
not be treated as a typical commodity and will be in a
class by itself. This has often been true throughout human
history and will remain true through the popping of the
bubbles.

Gold holds an unusual position in the minds of many
people around the world as a store of monetary value. Even
in the United States until the 20th century it was the most
common mode of monetary commerce. Hence, it is not
really a commodity in the same sense as wheat or zinc or oil.
Long-term, gold will behave very differently from other
commodities in terms of price. The values of other commodities are driven by commercial demand. Gold, on the
other hand, will be driven by the demand for a safe and rising place to store monetary value. In the short run, before
the bubbles pop, it may at times follow the prices of other
commodities as they rise and fall. But, as the bubbles start
to pop, gold's attraction as a traditional store for monetary
value will separate it from commercial commodities. Yes,
the demand for gold as jewelry will certainly fall since jewelry is a discretionary good, but that loss of demand will be
more than offset by a big increase in investment demand.
Furthermore, a great deal of gold jewelry that is purchased
in Asia or the Middle East is in large part for investment
purposes and can be easily re-sold if the money is needed.

For these reasons, gold is not part of our discussion of
commodities, but is covered earlier in this chapter.

Commodities—Metals such as Copper, Platinum and Silver

Metals such as nickel, zinc, and especially copper have huge industrial demand. Conversely, there is little investment demand for these metals. As the bubbles begin to burst, the industrial demand for these metals will fall precipitously. This will be especially true for copper, which has seen a massive increase in price in the last few years. Much of the demand that is driving copper's price has come from China which will see its demand for copper dramatically decline as its exports decline when the bubbles pop. In addition, there is clearly some speculative demand for copper that will dry up as its base industrial demand evaporates. In fact, the speculative demand will exit the market long before the full effect of declining industrial demand has been felt.

The advice regarding commodity metals is simple. You can play with them for a while and, if you are a good and/or lucky trader, you can make some money, but as soon as the bubbles start to pop, get out. When the bubbles pop, worldwide commodity metals prices will fall bigtime. Again, for U.S. produced commodities: as the dollar falls, the impact of falling commodity prices will be reduced.

Silver is a bit of a hybrid. It has some industrial demand, although the traditional demand for in photography is falling fast. However, like gold, it also has some investment demand because it has long been used as an alternative store of monetary value, second to gold. Like copper, when the bubbles pop, there will be a big decrease in industrial demand for silver and there will also be a big drop in demand for silver in jewelry as discretionary spending sharply declines. However, there will likely be some investment demand for silver. In fact, during the early part of 2006, silver outperformed gold. Silver, therefore, will likely do fine during the Bubblequake, but the safest bet with the highest likely long-term return in investment metals is still gold.

Platinum is in a similar position to silver in that it is in a hybrid position with both strong industrial demand and investment demand. However, much of the industrial demand is from catalytic converters in automobiles and, since autos are a capital good, it will see an unusually sharp decline in demand during the Bubblequake. Because of that, platinum is likely to be harder hit than silver, so we would recommend staying away from platinum as the bubbles begin to pop.

Commodities—Oil and Gas

Oil and gas will be a tale of two cities—one where the price is very high and one where the price is very low. In the United States, the price will be high, in the rest of the world, it will be low. This is one of the more unexpected effects of the popping of the bubbles, but it makes perfect sense. The price of oil has been driven up by the economic growth engine of the world: the U.S. economy. As that economy hits a major downturn, so will the price of oil. This is especially so because so much of the recent growth in oil prices is from Asian growth which is highly dependent upon massive exports to the United States. When the dollar falls dramatically in value and those exports drop substantially, the Asian economies, as mentioned before, will fall dramatically as well. And so will their consumption of oil.

However, in the United States, where we have to buy oil with dollars that have declined substantially in value, the price will be very high.

It will be strange that just across the border in Canada, the price for oil and natural gas will be low because Canadians can buy it with Canadian dollars. But, if we import it into the United States, the price will be very high because we have to pay for it with United States dollars. It will be one of those strange but true moments of the post bubble era and will last as long as it takes for the world's economies to balance their foreign trade and the foreign exchange markets (see Chapter 8).

Alternative Investments in Non-Euro Foreign Currencies

We don't recommend foreign currencies other than the euro. Although they may do well, they won't likely do much better than the euro and they could easily do far worse. If for some reason you really want to invest in other currencies, the yen and the Swiss franc will probably do the best. But, for pure investment purposes, stick with the euro. It's also the only one traded as an ETF on the New York Stock Exchange, making it an easy investment.

Betting Against the Stock Market

The stock market is in a bubble and heading for a fall. Many, many stock investors will get hurt, and there's no point in joining them. Either get out of the market now, or if you are experienced and confident enough, you can try your hand at betting against the market.

Most stock holders get happy when stock prices rise.

But seasoned investors know they can make money in *any* stock market, on its way up or on its way down. There are three tools for extracting profit from a falling stock market:

- Buying bear funds
- Buying put options
- Shorting stocks

The least risky way to bet against the market is to buy *bear market mutual funds*. These funds are often designed with varying degrees of emphasis on a down market. Some funds may be designed to track the market's decline. Other funds may be more aggressive and try to double the mar-

"All this for getting out when the getting was good."

ket's decline. It's like investing in income versus aggressive growth mutual funds, except that it's inverted. For suggestions of good places to purchase bear market mutual funds, please go to **www.americasbubbleeconomy.com/bearfunds.**

Another way to bet against the market that could produce higher returns, but could also be much more volatile, is to buy put options on stock market indexes such as the Standard & Poor's 500 index. The S&P index is known as the Spider—trading symbol is SPDR. Being based on the S&P 500, it is a broad market index that tracks the market as a whole. Such indexes are traded like stock and, as such, you can buy a put option against them. Of course, options by their nature are volatile and require a higher level of skill than most investors have. However, they also offer extremely high returns—like buying stocks on steroids. Your broker will have to qualify your account to buy options. Timing is key. Don't start until the market is beginning to burst. For more information on timing and more specifics on playing the options market, please go to **www.americasbubbleeconomy.com/ putoptions.**

Just as you can buy put options on indexes or even individual stocks, you can also *short stocks*. Clearly, this strategy will do well in a down market, but individual stocks are riskier than stock indexes. However, options are also more volatile and more difficult to manage. Hence, there may be a role for the more sophisticated investor to short stocks in industries that are likely to decline most significantly, such as capital goods. Again, timing is key. For more information on and more specifics on timing and on shorting stocks, please go to **www.americasbubbleeconomy .com/shortstock.**

> ### When the Bubbles Pop, the Stock Market Will Fall—So Why Will Stock Prices Skyrocket?
>
> One of the many strange aspects of the post-bubble economy will be adjusting to the new price of everything, including stocks. After the stock market dramatically falls in real terms, high inflation will make the **nominal price** of stocks soar. Finally, Dow 36,000 will actually become a reality! Of course, a pack of chewing gum will be selling for $7 by then, so don't get too excited.

A Safe Place to Stash Your Cash

In the short term, money markets are a fine place to keep your cash and maximize your returns. However, as we get closer to the Bubblequake, the risk of corporate bond and bank CD defaults increase, so we suggest eventually moving to short-term government debt mutual funds.

As mentioned before, never put any of your money in long-term bonds—the small premium is just not worth the risk. Keep an eye on our web site for more information on when to change your cash from money markets to short-term government debt. You can also sign up at the web site to receive e-mail alerts.

Creating Your Own Customized Investment Strategy

As they say on the TV ads, no one financial strategy is right for everybody. Creating a financial plan that is right for you means, first and foremost, determining your personal level of risk tolerance. In a traditional financial planning session, this assessment would look at two key factors: 1) How much money you have available to invest (the fewer assets you have, the lower your risk tolerance), and 2) Your age (the closer you are to retirement, the lower your risk tolerance).

To these, we'd like to add one more factor: 3) Your degree of confidence that America's Bubble Economy will, indeed, burst (the lower your confidence, the lower your risk tolerance).

Low-Risk Strategies

Let's say you are closing in on retirement (in your 50s) with a modest amount of investable assets (under $500,000) and modest concern that we might be right about the coming Bubblequake. That would put you into the low-risk tolerance category. Your potential investment options are as follows:

1. *Gold.* We recommend that the low-risk tolerance investor put 20 percent of his portfolio into gold now. Even now, a number of investment advisors from major brokerage firms are saying that putting 10 percent of your assets in gold as an inflation hedge may not be a bad idea. We recommend that the low-risk investor avoid leverage or margin. Over the next few years, it would be smart to increase the percentage of your portfolio in gold to 30 percent. Keep an eye on our web site at **www.americasbubbleeconomy.com/ goldtiming** for more information on when to increase your gold holdings. You can also sign up at the web site to receive e-mail alerts.

2. *Euros.* Diversifying your portfolio is always smart and a good way to do that is to buy some euros. We would

suggest putting 5 percent of your portfolio in nonmargined euro ETFs, or short-term, euro-denominated
bond fund.

3. *Bear funds*. We don't suggest putting any of your
money into bear funds, put options or in shorting
stocks. It's just too complicated and risky for the low
risk tolerant investor. You'll do just fine with your
gold and euros.

That's about it. As we said, we are trying to keep this
simple. For the low-risk tolerance investor, simplicity is
even more important. Keep the rest of your money in cash.

Medium-Risk Strategies

Let's say your retirement is still a ways off (in your 40s),
you have a modest amount of investable assets (under
$500,000), and you have a modest concern about the
likelihood of the coming Bubblequake. Or you are closing
in on retirement (in your 50s) with a large amount of
investable assets ($500,000 to $750,000), and have a
modest concern about the future. Or your retirement is
far off in the future, you have only modest investable
assets, but you have a very high concern about the coming
collapse of America's Bubble economy.

Here are your potential medium-risk investment
options:

1. *Gold*. We recommend that the medium-risk tolerance
investor put 30 percent of their portfolio into gold
now. We recommend leveraging the gold two to three
times to improve your returns. Over the next few

years, it would be smart to increase the percentage of your portfolio in gold to 40 to 50 percent. Keep an eye on our web site at **www.americasbubbleeconomy .com/goldtiming** for more information on when to increase your gold holdings. You can also sign up at the web site to receive e-mail alerts.

2. *Euros.* We suggest putting 15 percent of your portfolio in nonmargined euro ETFs.

3. *Bear funds.* We suggest putting 10 percent of your portfolio into bear funds. It is the easiest and safest way to bet against the market. Put options or shorting individual stocks are just too complicated and risky for the moderate risk tolerant investor. However, put options on market indexes are fine.

High-Risk Strategies

Your retirement is still off in the future (you are in your 40s), with a modest amount of investable assets (under $500,000), and you have a high concern about the coming mega money meltdown. Or you are close to retirement (in your 50s), with a large amount of investable assets ($750,000 to $1,000,000 or more), and you have a moderate belief that we may be right about the future economy. Or you are close to retirement, have little to invest or to lose, and you have a high level of belief that we are headed for a Bubblequake.

Here are your high-risk tolerance options:

1. *Gold.* We recommend that the high-risk tolerance investor put 40 percent of their portfolio into gold now. We recommend leveraging the gold up to three times to improve your returns. Over the next few

years, it would be smart to increase the percentage of your portfolio in gold to 60 to 70 percent. Keep an eye on our web site at **www.americasbubbleeconomy .com/goldtiming** for more information on when to increase your gold holdings. You can also sign up at the web site to receive e-mail alerts.

When the time is right, you may want to consider getting a fixed-rate line of credit or cash-out refinancing of real estate to buy gold and leveraged gold. Remember, high rates of inflation will rapidly lower the real cost of any fixed-rate mortgage you have.

2. *Euros*. We suggest putting 20 percent of your portfolio into euro ETFs with a 2× margin.

3. *Bear funds*. We suggest putting 15 percent of your portfolio into bear funds. It is the easiest and safest way to bet against the market. Put options, shorting individual stocks, and market indexes are alternatives for high-risk tolerant investors.

For more investment insights, there are a variety of smart people in the media today who are able to see beyond the rampant all-is-well cheerleading. For fun, yet hard-hitting analysis of the financial markets as a whole, as well as excellent insights about specific investments, *Newsweek* columnist Allan Sloan is among the best. Steve Pearlstein of the *Washington Post* is also one of the best financial markets analysts in the mainstream media, with an excellent ability to pick interesting topics often overlooked by other writers. Like Allan Sloan and Robert Samuelson, who we mentioned in the last chapter, Pearlstein is quite willing to take on conventional wisdom.

How Will Other Investment Vehicles, Such as Life Insurance and Collectibles Perform?

Life Insurance

As a rule, your best investment bets are gold, euros, and bear funds. Beyond that, here's how other investment vehicles will fair.

Term life insurance is fine; whole life insurance is not. Whole life or even hybrid life insurance (combination of term and whole) will do poorly simply because much of the money is invested in real estate, stocks, or other investments that will do poorly during the Bubblequake.

Term life insurance is fine since it is not really an investment. However, keep in mind that with very high inflation, the value of the pay-off amount will be greatly reduced. On the other hand, the real cost of the annual premium payments will also be reduced by inflation. Also keep in mind that once the bubbles burst, quite a few life insurance companies may go under and not be able to pay their claims. So once the value of the dollar begins to fall, keep a close eye on the health of your insurance company and increase your term life insurance to keep pace with inflation.

Art and Other Collectibles

All collectibles crash in value. In fact, if possible, postpone any collectibles purchases until after the bubble crash, when everything is at bargain basement prices. Not only will they be far cheaper, but your selection becomes huge because so many people need to sell their collectibles to raise money.

If you can bear to part with them, you would do best to begin selling off your collectibles now, before their market values dramatically drops. You can always buy back similar collectables at much lower prices later.

Are Diamonds Still a Girl's Best Friend?

Investment-grade diamonds will likely do OK, but non-investment diamonds will definitely fall in value due to declining demand for jewelry, which is very much a discretionary purchase, and will fall dramatically when the bubbles pop. Much of the increase in the value of investment-grade diamonds will come from the rise in the euro. Diamonds can be easily sold for euros and, hence, their price will go up in dollar terms as the euro rises.

Advice for European, Asian and Middle Eastern Investors

For All Non-U.S. Investors

Interestingly, much of the same advice we give to U.S. investors, we would also give to non-U.S. investors. Although the exact causes will be somewhat different in other parts of the world, the basic consequences will be the same for most of the world's economies—declining asset values and higher interest rates and inflation rates. Hence, stay away from local stock markets, stay away from real estate, and don't buy long term or fixed rate debt. Government debt in the major industrialized nations is relatively safe in the short term, but expect high inflation in many parts of the world. Gold and euros are good investments and betting against most major stock markets is also a good long-term bet.

For European Investors

The European economy will be hit hard by the meltdown of the U.S. economy. This will put dramatic downward pressure on European stocks and real estate. In addition, most European investors will be taking huge losses on their dollar denominated U.S. investments (except those who read this book and got out in time). Many of these investment groups—pension funds, life insurance companies, investment banks—will be facing bankruptcy or will certainly have far less money to invest. The bankruptcies and lack of funds will severely damage the European investment climate and the European economies. In fact, in many ways, since they are America's bankers, they will be hit far harder than U.S. investors.

Because of these conditions, the asset covering commandments we stated earlier are equally important for European investors. However, one obvious difference is investments in the euro. Since Europeans don't use dollars for their consumption expenses, they cannot benefit from investing in euros. Instead, selling their dollar-denominated investments over the next couple of years becomes your Asset Covering Commandment #6.

Buying gold and betting against the stock market are quite viable strategies for making large returns. Unfortunately, the extra profits that Americans will make from the sale of gold bought at a low price in dollars and sold into euros will obviously not flow to Europeans. Since an investment in gold is also essentially an investment in euros (because gold is easy to sell for euros), this is where a large portion of the profits from gold will be for Americans. Unfortunately, Europeans will not be able to benefit from this extra profit source. However, gold will still be an excellent investment for Europeans, just not as profitable as for Americans who bought the gold at low prices with dollars.

Betting against the stock market using the same tools as described earlier, bear mutual funds, shorting stocks and put options—to the extent that they are available on the various European markets—are just as profitable for Europeans as for Americans. European stock markets will be hurt as much or more than U.S. stock markets. However, since the dollar will be declining substantially, betting against American stock markets will not be a good option.

Europeans who have invested properly have the option of consuming some of their wealth in dollars by traveling to the United States or buying U.S. goods. Unfortunately for the United States, most Europeans will have lost much of their money, especially anything invested in the United States, so we can't count on a big influx of investment or purchases from Europeans after the bubbles pop. But, for those few who made the right investment moves, their euros can be used in traveling to the United States or buying U.S. goods. So, even if Europeans can't entirely benefit from the rise of the euro, to the extent they can travel to the United States or buy U.S. goods, they can get a partial benefit. For those few inclined to do so, they could also take their euro profits, move to the United States, and "cash them in."

Asian Investors

The major difference between Asian investors and European or American investors is that the Asian economies and

Asian investment markets will be hit much harder. The massive loss of exports will be truly devastating to Asian economies and their investment and real estate markets will be damaged proportionally. In addition, the losses that Chinese and Japanese governments will take on their dollar investments will cause their economic situations to deteriorate further. Add to those losses, a very large Japanese federal deficit that will be extremely difficult to manage once the bubbles pop, and you have a recipe for a major economic setback for the entire Asian region.

Our advice for Asian investors is similar to that for Europeans. Follow all the asset covering commandments mentioned earlier in this chapter and add a sixth commandment to sell all of your dollar denominated investments over the next couple of years. We should also note that since Asia is still very much in an economic boom currently, there is still money to be made in Asian stock markets and real estate—*if* you can be sure to sell out before the American bubbles pop. Also, as in any boom that is nearing its end, there is likely to be great volatility, as we have already seen in Asian stock markets in 2006. So, much more than the Europeans or Americans, there is still likely money to be made in Asia, but be careful. When the bubbles pop, their effect will be much greater in Asia than in the U.S. or Europe.

Profitable investment options for Asians are similar to those for Europeans, but with more emphasis on gold than on betting against the stock market. This is partly due to a greater interest in gold on the part of many Asian investors and also because there are fewer options for betting against the Asian stock markets than in Europe or the United States.

Middle Eastern Investors

The major difference between Middle Eastern and other investors is obviously oil. The big impact from the popping of America's Bubble Economy on the Middle East will be to dramatically drive down the price of oil—something that would be totally unexpected, but makes perfect sense. The price of oil has been driven up by the economic growth engine of the world, the U.S. economy, and as that economy hits a major downturn, so will the price of oil. This is especially so because so much of the recent growth in oil prices is from Asian growth which is highly dependent upon massive exports to the United States. When the dollar falls dramatically in value and those exports drop substantially, the Asian economies, as mentioned before, will fall dramatically as well. And so will their consumption of oil.

The falling dollar will further dampen the oil market by dramatically raising the price of oil imported into the United States. Gasoline in the United States could easily reach $7 a gallon or more and when combined with a major economic downturn, U.S. consumption of imported oil will fall dramatically, as will the worldwide price of oil.

This huge fall in the price of oil after the bubbles pop will clearly devastate Middle Eastern economies, stock markets and real estate. So, just like other non-U.S. investors, Middle Eastern investors should follow our five asset covering commandments and add the sixth one—over the next couple of years, sell your dollar denominated investments.

Our advice to Middle Eastern investors is very similar to Asian investors. Since the Middle East is still in an economic boom from the high price of oil, there is still money to be made in the real estate and stock markets. However, as in any boom that is nearing its end, there is likely to be great volatility, as we have already seen in Middle Eastern stock markets in 2006. So, like the Asians, there is still likely some money to be made in the Middle East before America's bubbles pop, but, be careful, the bubbles will pop and their effect will be much greater in the Middle East and Asia than in the United States or Europe.

In terms of making money, the options for Middle Eastern investors are similar to Europeans, but with more emphasis on gold than on betting against the stock market. This is partly due to a greater interest in gold on the part of many Asian investors and also because there are fewer options for betting against the Middle Eastern stock markets than in Europe or the United States.

In Times of Major Investment Downturns, Money Does Not Get Moved from One Asset to Another. It Goes to Money Heaven.

Many people believe that if the U.S. economy sours, investors will simply move their money out of their U.S. assets and into other safer assets in Europe or Asia. In fact, they will just lose their money.

This is not surprising. When the stock market crashed in 1929, did all the money that was in the stock market prior to the crash simply move out of stocks and into bonds? No, most of it was lost. It went to money heaven.

When financial changes are small, assets do indeed move from one class of assets to another. But, when a crisis hits, the money doesn't move, it simply disappears. It doesn't move because there is nothing to move. It takes only a small fraction of investors selling any asset to drive down its value enormously. If 20% of the people holding a stock decide to sell that stock, its value does not merely fall 20%, it goes down a whole lot more. The people who don't sell early simply lose their money. They don't get to move it to another asset class.

When the Bubblequake hits, foreign investors will not simply move their money out of the United States. Instead, they will lose most of their money now in U.S. assets, just as the central banks of China and Japan will lose most of the money they invested in buying dollars to support its value. They won't get to move their money, either. It will simply disappear.

Chapter SIX

Gold for People Who Hate Gold

By Bubble Expert Eric Janszen

The one and only time I have written on the subject of gold was September 2001 in an article written for my website **www.iTulip.com.** I concluded:

One can buy physical gold now for around $270 and have gold provide the same "fundamental strength" to one's personal balance sheet as it provides the IMF's. As a long-term investment I conclude that its value is far more doubtful. The environment for capital appreciation is more likely to persist long term than not. Progress marches on. One is better off owning an index of stocks that will tend to grow in line with inevitable growth of the world economy, in spite of occasional setbacks. Still, it's hard to go wrong with a small gold bullion position. Gold is now trading near 13 percent of its inflation-adjusted peak price of $1,973 (in 1999 dollars) whereas U.S. stocks as a class are trading at a premium rarely seen, even after recent declines.

It is possible that the price of gold will fall the remaining 13 percent to zero and the DJIA will rise to 36,000 in the next few years as some predict. But is the collapse of the price of gold the remaining 13 percent toward zero more or less likely than a return of stock prices to their historical P/E ratios? Is not a counter-cyclical return of the price of gold relative to the DJIA likely to revert toward a price ratio closer to one to one from the current ratio of 37 to one?

If gold indeed falls another 50 percent to $135 you have paid a small risk premium for owning the world's oldest and most widely held financial catastrophe insurance, and a lot less than the 87 percent you have lost investing (speculating) in the widely touted New Economy stocks represented in the iTulip.com Index when we first warned you to not buy them back in January 1999.

Since then, gold has increased from $270 to $581 as of this writing, five years later. Any reader heeding this advice not only has not had to pay to hold gold as insurance, they have benefited from a 115 percent increase in the value of the insurance. That represents a 17 percent compound annual rate of interest over five years. Who says gold doesn't earn interest?

I arrived at this conclusion in 2001 from research on the pros and cons of gold investing combined with intuition developed from many years of personal experience with gold investing going back to childhood. I'll touch briefly on the childhood experience first, discuss the research second and conclude the chapter with ideas about where gold is likely to go from here.

Gold in the Family

Writing my original analysis on gold in 2001 required soul searching. I questioned my ability to remain objective with a personal history with gold going back to adolescence. I explored my emotional and sentimental attachment to gold that might incline me to make a case for buying it.

My interest in gold started when, at age 17 in 1975, my father and my uncle introduced me to gold. Before I get into that, a brief history of gold leading up to that very turbulent period in history.

The world's central banks eliminated direct ties between their currencies and gold on March 15, 1968. Three years later, an executive order by Richard Nixon kept foreign holders of U.S. dollars from redeeming them for gold held by the U.S. Treasury. This act was a kind of default in the view of several central banks, especially France's. Private gold ownership by U.S. citizens was legalized less than two years later, on the last day of the year 1974.

For those readers who are entirely new to gold's recent history, you may be surprised to learn that for 41 years U.S. citizens were not allowed to own gold bullion. On April 5, 1933, U.S. President Franklin Delano Roosevelt issued Presidential Executive Order 6102 calling in gold owned for the purpose of "hoarding." Private citizens were paid for their confiscated gold with paper dollars at the going rate of $20.67 per ounce. The Treasury then set a new price of gold at $35 per ounce, thus devaluing the dollar and boosting the gold-backed dollar money supply by close to 30 percent. The purpose was to halt the persistent deflation that was crippling the U.S. economy.

Forty-one years later, with Executive Order 11825 on December 31, 1974, President Gerald Ford repealed the Executive Order that Roosevelt used to call in gold in 1933. In 1977, Congress further removed the president's authority to regulate gold transactions, during any period of national emergency other than war. In the three years that passed between the delinking of gold from the dollar and the legalization of private gold ownership, my father and uncle anticipated the coming change in gold ownership law and discussed the merits of buying gold.

I remember my father's phone calls back and forth with my uncle. They concluded that the Fed was likely to succumb to political pressure to overextend the money supply. My father was a Harvard-trained physicist. Born and raised in Texas, he had a healthy distrust of government. He and my uncle hypothesized that pressure on politicians to fund everything voters and special interests wanted, and some things many didn't want such as the Vietnam War, was likely to induce politicians to abuse their new ability to create money freely without the constraints imposed by either a gold standard or settlement of foreign debts from Treasury gold reserves. Monetization of debt and price inflation were likely to follow. They seemed especially certain that the Fed might print money to fund the war in Vietnam rather than engage in the more fiscally responsible yet politically difficult act of raising taxes. They also worried that some unforeseeable crisis might occur to cause the money supply to grow in an uncontrolled fashion. My father and uncle bought gold in early 1975 to hedge these risks.

"I know there's the myth of the autonomous Fed
... [short laugh] and when you go up for confirmation
some Senator may ask you about your friendship with
the President. Appearances are going to be important,
so you can call Ehrlichman to get messages to me, and
he'll call you."

—Richard Nixon to Arthur Burns,
John Ehrlichman, *Witness to Power*, New York, 1982.

Of course, eight years earlier my father and uncle
could not have known that such dealings between the
Fed and the White House were going on, but the evidence was there and they decided to act on it. They
bought gold.

The decision was very contrary to mainstream thinking at the time. Much as today, inflation was reported at a
rate that did not accord with the price changes that the
average U.S. citizen could observe at the supermarket or
the gas station. Also, in the minds of investors, gold was
way out of date as an asset class. New financial products,
such as stock mutual funds and hedge funds, were the
place to go. The consensus among financial markets pun-
dits and economists was that gold had no future at all as a
personal financial asset. The Chairman of the Bank for
International Settlements (BIS), for example, proclaimed
in 1972 that gold without demand from central banks as a
monetary asset was free to fall from its pre free-market
fixed price of $35 to its true market value as an industrial
commodity, "around $7.50 per ounce." Eight years after
making that statement, gold was trading at nearly 100
times the price the Chairman predicted.

What the Research Showed

Gold did not, however, go up in a straight line. It followed the usual progression of an asset bubble. From an average price of $161 in 1975 (when gold became legal to own in the United States), the price declined to $124 in 1976, rose to $147 in 1977, and to $193 in 1978. For the first three years of the previous bull market in gold, the percentage price increase was less than the percentage price increase that occurred between at the start of the current bull market, between 2001 and 2006. During that time, inflation was rising rapidly while the stock market remained more or less flat, except that adjusted for inflation, the stock market declined significantly. As the chart below shows, the best trade for a trader at the time was to sell stocks and buy gold (see Figure 6.1).

Good call on my father's part to buy gold when he

Figure 6.1 Average Annual Dow and Gold Values and Inflation Rate 1974–1983

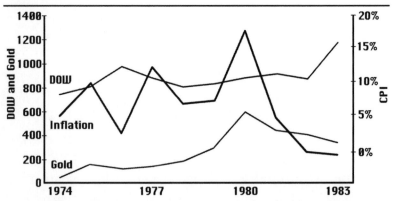

Comparing the annual average price of gold, the growth of the Dow, and the CPI inflation level, we can see that gold prices tend not to track inflation year to year, but rather anticipate long term inflation trends.

did. Unfortunately, he did not see the gold price at the top of the market as a bubble in 1980 and held on to it, even as the Paul Volcker Fed raised interest rates into double-digit levels and threw the U.S. economy into the worst recession since The Great Depression. Figure 6.2 shows the impact on inflation of Volcker's tightening, as well as the recession it created in 1980.

My parents passed away in the early 1990s. I sold the gold that I inherited, all but one Mexican 50 Peso gold coin that I kept for good luck and invested in the stock market. Gold was trading then at around $350 ($474 in 2006 dollars). The Dow Jones Industrial Average (DJIA) spent the year 1992 around 3,200 and NASDAQ around 600. From then on, we know where the DJIA and NAS-DAQ went: up, up, and away, until the crash of 2000. Gold

Figure 6.2 Average Consumer Price Inflation 1975–1980

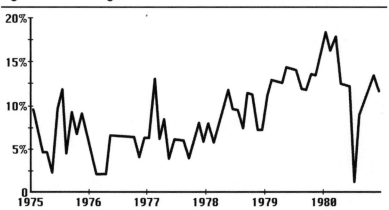

Although the annual average level of CPI inflation from 1975 to 1980 has been volatile from year to year, the price of gold rose steadily as the market was betting that the long-term structural problems that were causing the inflation would not be fixed with short term band-aids that reduced inflation in some years.

declined with intermittent rallies to its aforementioned low of $256 in 2001 over the same period.

My personal experience investing in gold in the past had been positive. As Managing Director of a seed-stage angel investment firm in the late 1990s, I had a good sense of the excesses that were happening in the stock market at the time. I started a web site called iTulip.com to parody poorly conceived Internet companies that were getting financed at the time. On the site, I predicted a crash in the early part of 2000, a prediction for which the *New York Times,* among others, gave me credit. At the same time, I was already trying to figure out what the Fed and policymakers in Washington were likely to do after the inevitable crash. Drawing heavily from the Levy Institute, among others, I concluded that a post-bubble reflation program in the form of rate cuts, tax cuts and fresh liquidity was coming. The previous reflation program, the one that followed the real estate crash in the early 1990s that put the U.S. banking system on hold for about six months, was the monetary fuel that led to the stock market bubble that started around 1995. The question to me in 1999 was, where was the liquidity going to go this time? My deduction was that commodities in general—and specifically gold—was a likely candidate.

The gold price increased more than 100 percent since my one and only prediction in September 2001. Comparing the 1974 to 1984 period with the 2001 to 2006 period shows marked similarities. As Mark Twain once said, "History does not repeat, but it does echo."

In the 1974 to 1984 graph shown in Figure 6.2, we use the Federal Reserve as our source for inflation data for that period but use Gillespie Research data for the 2001 to 2006 period shown in the chart below (see Figure 6.3).

Figure 6.3 Average Annual Dow and Gold Values and Inflation Rate 2000–2006

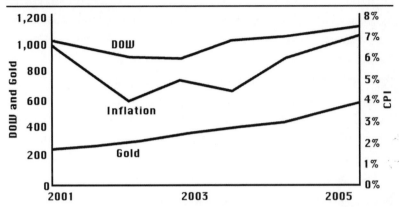

The data collected for the CPI inflation index and the methods of analysis used to arrive at the numbers reported by the Bureau of Labor Statistics (BLS) have changed several times since 1980. If the same methods of calculation are used today as were used in 1980, CPI inflation averaged 7% in 2005 versus 3.5% as reported by the BLS. Inflation growing from 4% to 7% between 2002 and 2005 helps explain why the price of gold increased from $270 to $580 during the period.

The government's methods of inflation indexing, collection, and analysis have been modified so much since the Nixon administration, most notably under the Clinton and Bush II administrations, that it's necessary to use Gillespie's ShadowStats.com data to get an accurate picture of what's going on. Use the Fed's current data and recent commodities price increases do not fit any rational pricing model. However, plug in Gillespie Research's numbers, and the price increases in commodities, including gold, begins to make sense. While the commodities markets have not been fooled by the dubious government statistics, bond yields are lower than expected given the real rate of inflation. There are two possible explanations.

One is that ongoing "vendor financing" of U.S. consumption by Asia through the purchases of U.S. treasury and agency debt are artificially lowering bond yields. The alternative conclusion is that, on a risk-adjusted basis, a 10-year U.S. treasury bond is still considered a "good deal" at 4.5 percent even with inflation running at 7 percent.

U.S. citizens were not permitted to own gold bullion for 42 years, from 1933 until January 1975. After that, the last gold bull market began. It got off to a slow start. Private and institutional investors had not had any experience investing in gold for 42 years. Plus, right after the gold market reopened in the United States in 1975, inflation fell dramatically, from 10 percent to 2.5 percent and with it the price of gold. Even the following year when inflation shot back up to 12.5 percent, the price of gold increased only modestly, as market participants were slow to catch on to what was happening. But gold continued to climb modestly even as inflation fell again between 1977 and 1978 as the first wave of buyers—the early adopters—started to show up. Then, a couple of years into the bull market, the second wave of buyers entered the market and gold took off in its second stage of growth in 1979, even though inflation was relatively tame that year compared to recent spikes. That price rise anticipated the spike in inflation that occurred in 1980 when both inflation and gold peaked in its final bubble wave in 1980. Back then you couldn't find an investment book that didn't tell you to buy gold and other hard assets and stay away from stocks. That was the exact opposite of what investors should have been doing because in came Paul Volcker to take over the Fed from Nixon's pal Burns. Volcker put the hammer down, cranking interest rates up in 2 percent rate hikes. None of this baby-step stuff that the Fed's doing today. Inflation collapsed from 18 percent in 1980 to –2.5 percent in 1983. The U.S. economy fell into a deep recession for most of that period.

What does this mean for us today? After a 20 year bear market that started in 1980 and ended in 2001, investors have been as slow to catch on to the new bull market in gold, as well as other commodities including silver and platinum, as they were after the previous bear market in gold, or rather nonmarket in gold, as U.S. citizens were not allowed to own it. The DJIA has for the past several years been rising, much as it did between 1978 and 1981 when inflation and gold were also rising, but in inflation-adjusted terms in both periods the DJIA declined. The painful period of adjustment that the Volcker Fed created set the United States up for a long and massive expansion that, during its healthy prebubble phase from 1982 to 1995, saw the DJIA grow in inflation-adjusted terms by nearly 400 percent.

The crucial question is whether the rising price of commodities is again predicting a future rise in inflation. I believe that it is. We will see this inflation spike at some point and the price of gold with it. The second wave of gold investors is getting on board as we enter the next phase of the bull market, not only gold but silver and platinum as well.

At some point commodities will also reach a bubble phase. The bookstore shelves will again be stuffed with books that tell you to buy hard assets, and everyone from you mail carrier to your neighbor will be lecturing you about gold. Then it will be time to get out.

Most likely with a change of political administration, the source of inflation that is driving gold up will be addressed by the Fed in a manner similar to Volcker's. This time the job will be to put an end to the cycle of asset bubbles that have been driving the economy since around 1995. When this happens, the United States will once again go through a painful transition but will, in the end, come out ahead for the reasons it has in the past.

Now that gold is trading at more than twice the lowest price of $255.95 it reached in April 2001, is gold now expensive? Is it too late to buy it?

It is important to keep in mind when discussing the price of gold not to confuse the nominal price with the real price. The nominal price is the price not adjusted for inflation, its "real" price. To create a true historical context for the price of gold, we need to pick a grounding point for the gold price, its price at the bottom of the previous cycle the day that U.S. citizens were allowed to buy gold on the open market, January 1, 1975. The spot price of gold was $176. In 2001 when the price of gold bottomed at $256, the purchasing power of $176 had decline due to inflation so that $608 was needed to purchase items of the same value. So the price of gold at $256 in 2001 was an incredibly low price in real terms: $256 in 2001 was $74 in 1976 dollars. Now that's cheap! You can see why I didn't think I was sticking my neck out to recommend buying it. What about now?

Now let's look at the peak gold price. There was a bubble in the price of gold that peaked in 1980 at $870, or $2,200 in 2006 dollars. That means that today, even though gold is trading at more than twice the 2001 market cycle bottom price of $256, at $580 gold is still trading at less than one-third of its real price at the previous inflation cycle top. Another point to consider is that the asset bubble cycle tends to increase the degree of both the bottom and top price of the asset price cycles, as we've seen in housing prices which recently peaked.

Why do I expect a big rise in inflation? There are several factors but the most important was the same as the factor that was driving inflation in the 1970s that led to the peak for gold in 1980: energy.

While there is a broad range of opinions on whether energy prices will increase sharply or gradually from here, few argue that energy prices are due to decline. Ignoring the risks of a rapid increase resulting from geopolitical tensions in this discussion, assume that the recent Army Corps of Engineers report is correct and that the price of oil, which has increased 300 percent from less than $20 per barrel to over $60 since gold began its rise, continues to rise to $200 per barrel over the next five years due to growing demand and limited supply (see Figure 6.4).

My expectation is that the next inflation cycle peak will take the nominal price of gold above the previous

Figure 6.4   Spot Oil Price

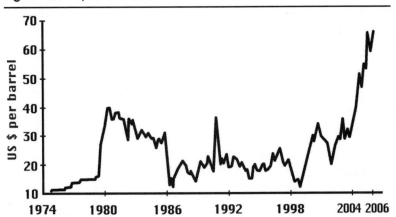

A major driver of inflation is the price of energy, especially oil. The price of gold tracks the price of oil fairly closely over time. If oil price increases are sharp or sustained, the price of gold tends to rise sharply or in a sustained way, as well.

$1,714 inflation-adjusted peak price. I expect a gold price in the range of $2,500 to $3,000 in 2006 dollars within the next five years. The dollar will have depreciated considerably by then, accounting for much of the nominal gold price increase. So before you get excited about "making money" on gold, keep in mind that this increase will largely be the result of several factors that are likely to drive the nominal price of gold up, but keep real gains in the price of gold more modest; in fact, nominal gains in the gold price may have already occurred.

One gold price indicator that bears watching is the ratio of the price of gold to the price of stocks. As the chart below shows, the two asset classes have historically had a strong inverse price correlation (see Figure 6.5).

Investor sentiment today, much as during the early days in the last bull market in gold, is still very small. While the price has increased significantly over the past few years, this is a recent development. The current generation of investors has only known gold as an out-of-date asset that has been declining in price for decades, until recently. The process of buying gold is foreign to these investors, although the creation of new gold products, such as gold *Exchange Traded Funds* (ETFs) like GLD, make the process of purchasing gold more familiar. Investors can buy gold as shares of an EFT using their brokerage account, much as they purchase stocks, mutual or index fund shares. No visits to the coin store to deal with quirky coin store owners or dealing with the high transaction costs of buying and selling gold over the Internet. Still, gold is generally viewed as a pessimist's investment, when in fact it is really nothing more than a form of insurance against a number of increasingly likely problems.

Figure 6.5 Ratio of Dow to Gold Price

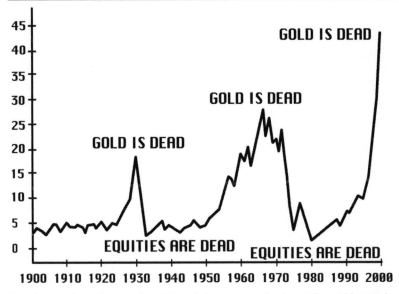

Investor sentiment toward gold tends to run counter to sentiment toward stocks. The ratio in the price of gold to the price of the DOW is an indicator of this relationship. When the DOW peaked after a long bull market that ended in the year 2000, and gold bottomed after a 20 year long bear market, gold appeared to investors to be a "dead" investment. Conversely, in 1980 when the DOW had been through a 14 year bear market and gold was hitting all time highs, investors believed stocks were "dead." These cycles of sentiment are driven by long-term structural changes in the macro-economy, geopolitics and financial markets.

Other traditional hedges against inflation are less likely to work as well in this inflation cycle as in the last. Real estate, for example, has already experienced a major price bubble itself, and housing prices tend to not do well during inflationary periods due to the high interest rates that typically occur at the same time. Gold is not, however, the only precious metal to rise over the past several years. Both silver and platinum have increased by an even

195

Figure 6.6   Price of Silver 2000–2006

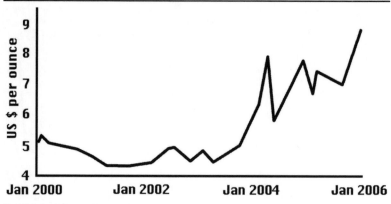

Gold is not the only precious metal that increased in price in line with rising inflation between 2001 and 2006. Silver increased even more, rising more than 100% from around $4 per ounce in 2001 to more than $9 in 2006.

larger percentage, and a diversification among gold, silver and platinum is wise (see Figure 6.6).

Conclusion

My perspective on gold is colored by personal history. My father and uncle successfully timed a purchase of gold based on a prediction of how the government was likely to behave. Their error was to not foresee the 20-plus-year decline in gold after Fed Chairman Paul Volcker put the United States through a wrenching three-year recession in order to wring inflation out of the economy and the Greenspan Fed pushed interest rates lower while government spending declined.

Now it appears as though the United States is making many of the same errors that were made during the era of Nixon and Burns, including massive government deficits, underfunded entitlements and an unpopular war that the government cannot fund with higher taxes or special bonds for the purpose. On top of that, the world economy, and its demand for commodities is growing rapidly, most notably in China. Even Japan, which has suffered from deflation for over a decade, is starting to see some inflation. The Bank of Japan is starting to raise interest rates for the first time in more than 13 years.

To me, five years after my previous prediction, all roads still lead to inflation, whether due to energy costs, unfunded deficits or dollar currency risks. I still recommend an asset allocation of 10 percent to 15 percent of assets to hedge this risk. While I'm sticking to a predicted peak price of $2,500 to $3,000 (in 2006 dollars), the important factor to keep in mind is market psychology. As gold approaches its peak price, so will the degree of hype around it. Don't be afraid to miss the very top. No point in holding on to your gold insurance after the storm has passed.

Chapter SEVEN

Survive and Thrive

Find the Best Businesses and Jobs
When the Bubbles Burst

The fall of America's Bubble Economy will shake up many industries, drive businesses into bankruptcy, derail countless careers, and force dramatic numbers of workers into temporary unemployment. It will also create thousands of successful companies that don't currently exist, lead all sorts of people to rethink their life's work, and make many, many alert entrepreneurs and investors fabulously wealthy.

Depending on how well you face facts and reposition yourself in the next couple of years, you could be in for a rude awakening, a sleepy slowdown, or dream-come-true prosperity. Despite the widespread problems that most U.S. businesses and workers will face, there are real opportunities for tremendous financial success for those who, by fate or forethought, happen to end up in the right place at the right time.

Later in this chapter, we show you a few ways you can join them, but first we need to deliver the bad news before it catches you off guard.

This Ain't Your Daddy's Economic Slowdown

This is not the 1970s. What we tend to think of when we think of life in an economic slowdown is not what we are about to get. This one is going to be bigger, badder, deeper, and longer than what we've seen before.

To understand why, we need to take a closer look at three important sectors of the U.S. economy (see Figure 7.1):

- *Capital Goods Sector*: Cars, construction, major industrial equipment, etc.

Figure 7.1   Three Economic Sectors

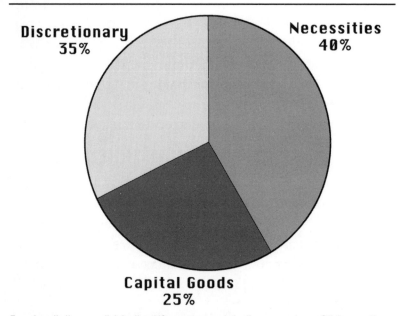

For simplicity, we divide the US economy into three sectors. Of these, the Capital Goods Sector will be hit the hardest in the coming Bubblequake, followed by Discretionary Spending. The Necessities Sector will also sustain a blow, but will hold up the best when the bubbles pop.

- *Discretionary Spending Sector*: Restaurants, entertainment, travel, and discretionary consumer goods, etc.

- *Necessities Sector*: Basic food, shelter, clothing, energy, government services, healthcare, etc.

Typically, in an economic downturn, such as the recession of the 1970s, we can expect the Capital Goods Sector to slow significantly, the Discretionary Spending Sector to decline somewhat, and the Necessities Sector to mostly be spared—under normal conditions.

By this point, you've probably guessed that conditions during and after the bubbles collapse are anything but normal. If you hope your business survives and thrives in the coming Bubblequake, or if you would like to keep your current job or gear up for an even better one, the following insights may shed some light on what to expect in each of the three economic sectors.

For more details about major industries within each economic sector, please visit the following links:

- www.americasbubbleeconomy.com/necessities

- www.americasbubbleeconomy.com/ discretionaryspending

- www.americasbubbleeconomy.com/capitalgoods

Customized Analysis for Your Specific Industry, Business, or Investment Goals

The authors and their economic experts and experienced business valuators can apply rigorous economic analysis to a variety of industries and businesses, based on the ideas presented in this book. Individual investors, investment bankers and other investment professionals can also benefit from personalized consulting to suit their particular needs. Country-specific analysis can be customized for rapidly changing conditions in the United States, Europe, Asia, or the Middle East.

For more information, please contact The Foresight Group at 800–994–0018.

The Capital Goods Sector (Autos, Construction, Major Industrial Equipment, Etc.)

Super-high interest rates, coupled with a big economic slowdown, will be very bad news for the Capital Goods Sector. As we discussed earlier, our huge accumulation of government debt, plus our other foreign and domestic debt, will drive up interest rates to unprecedented levels when the bubbles pop. High interest rates will make borrowing money very expensive for individuals and, more importantly, for businesses. High interest rates will be nothing short of an unmitigated disaster for the Capital Goods Sector, which depends on customers having access to low-cost capital. And high interest rates will make recovery after the Bubblequake far longer and more difficult than in previous recessions.

How Businesses Will Fare in the Capital Goods Sector

We won't dress it up for you. The bottom line for business owners in the Capital Goods Sector is not pretty. If you can sell now, you should.

No one can predict exactly when the Bubblequake will hit, but even if it takes another five years, the marketplace for your business is unlikely to improve much, if at all. Prices for businesses are pretty good now and they aren't going to get significantly better any time soon. In fact, the values of Capital Goods Sector companies will decrease substantially as we get closer to the final fall. So if you have a business in the automotive, construction, industrial equipment, or any other Capital Goods industry, the longer you wait to get out, the more vulnerable you will be to significant loss.

Given that we don't expect the bubbles to pop for another couple of years, you could use that time to improve your company so you can sell it for the best possible price. If you were planning to sell your company in five years, you might want to move up your time frame a bit. If you were planning to sell in 10 years, definitely move up that goal.

What will you do after you sell? Options include using your proceeds to invest in the huge wealth-building opportunities discussed in Chapters 5 and 6, or to buy or start up another business that is better positioned to survive and flourish in the post-bubble economy (some possibilities are discussed later in this chapter).

Your Job Prospects in the Capital Goods Sector

As hard as it may be to sell one's business, it can be even harder to quit your job and train for another career. Unlike selling a business, which at least provides the possibility of getting some cash, quitting a job usually means walking away, cold turkey, from a paycheck. And in the Capital

Goods Sector of the economy, that paycheck may be quite a bit better than jobs elsewhere in the economy. So we are fully aware that you may have no interest in leaving a lucrative job in order to take what may be a lower paying position.

Still, you might as well know the cold, hard facts: Jobs in Capital Goods industries will be the worst hit by the coming Bubblequake and there isn't much you can do to protect yourself other than to gear up to move on. Your best bet may be to rethink your career, with an eye toward joining an industry that will do far better when the bubbles burst.

If a major career makeover is not your style, you may want to consider making a move to a more stable area within your current industry. For example, if you work in the construction industry—which will take a truly terrible hit—you may find that moving into repair-oriented work, rather than new construction, will keep you busy while others sit at home. Of course, many construction workers will also get this idea after the bubbles pop, so the sooner you begin your transition, the better.

Learning vehicle repair will also keep you employed, as will retraining for a job in the other sectors of the economy that will also be hit, but not as hard as the Capital Goods Sector.

The Discretionary Spending Sector (Travel, Restaurants, Entertainment—and a Big Surprise)

As you might guess, when the going gets tough, Americans are simply not going to run out to the mall every night after work (if they have work) and squander their limited cash and very limited credit on one more high-priced designer handbag or the latest CD. Discretionary spending, is . . . well, discretionary. And many items and activities we currently enjoy will simply be off our shopping lists after the bubbles pop. This will certainly slow many businesses to a crawl and force others completely out of the game.

The impact of the coming Bubblequake won't rock the Discretionary Spending Sector of the economy as much as it will Capital Goods. Here's why. Some people will still have money and they will keep spending their money, only at a lower level than before. So, instead of discretionary spending disappearing altogether, people will simply buy lower priced discretionary items.

Take restaurants, for example. Once the bubbles pop, far fewer people and businesses will have money to spend on eating out. That will certainly affect all restaurants. But there will still be some people and businesses that do have money and will be quite happy to go to restaurants, as long as they don't have to spend as much as they used to. So the restaurant industry will continue to be a huge industry in the United States, but business will shift dramatically toward the lower end.

To a large extent, the exact same thing will happen throughout the Discretionary Spending Sector. Instead of brand names, we'll buy bargains. We will still buy stuff we don't absolutely have to have, we'll just buy less of it and at lower prices.

The Big Surprise: Discretionary Spending Accounts for a Lot More of the Overall U.S. Economy Than Ever Before

The big surprise about the current U.S. economy is just how wealthy we are. We routinely spend huge amounts of money and credit on things we really don't need, and so a whole lot more of our current economy is in the Discretionary Spending Sector than ever has been before. That means, once incomes and credit cards are in short supply, a much greater percentage of the U.S. economy is going to feel the pain than ever before.

This is an entirely new situation for us. Back in the 1920s, when the nation was much less wealthy heading into the Great Depression, discretionary spending represented a smaller portion of our overall economy. So when the stock market bubble crashed in 1929 and the economy took a major downturn, the large dip in discretionary spending had less impact because it just didn't make up that large a part of the economy. Other industries took a big hit, but people still had to eat basic food and buy basic clothing, so most of these industries just kept on going.

A very different situation exists today. So much of what we currently buy (and that keeps our economy going) we can easily do without. We may not like forgoing a trip to Whole Foods or Wegman's where we can select from a huge range of expensive goodies, but if we have to, we certainly can and will survive on cheaper foods from low-priced stores. We may not like to skip the latest, high-priced fashions, but if we have to, we can easily shop at lower-level and discount stores. We can also survive quite nicely without $100,000 kitchen and bathroom makeovers, complete with granite countertops and stainless steel appliances. Once incomes and assets begin to evaporate and we need to conserve cash, Americans very quickly (although not very happily) learn to manage without these pricey pleasures.

Of course, if spending on lavish food, clothing, and housing can easily be cut, and if this kind of spending represents a big chunk of America's current economy, then the impact of these changes will be very, very negative indeed. While the Discretionary Spending Sector will be hit less hard than the Capital Goods Sector, the fact that Discretionary Spending has become such a big part of the current U.S. economy means a downturn in this sector will greatly accelerate and deepen the Bubblequake, as well as slow our post-bubble recovery.

Businesses and Jobs in the Discretionary Spending Sector

We've already mentioned how a slowdown in the Discretionary Spending Sector harms many businesses in the fancy food, high-end clothing, fine-dining, and home improvement industries. The travel industry will take an even greater hit. Leisure travel will be in very bad shape, and travel overseas will face a double whammy as the buying power of the dollar falls. Business travel will suffer, as well. Because of the high costs and low value of the dollar, only the most important overseas business travel will occur. With our imports way down and our exports low, due to the major recession around the world, there simply won't be as much need for business travel overseas.

Domestic business travel will also decrease due to the sharp slowdown in the economy and the cost-cutting mindset that most companies will be forced to adopt.

And domestic leisure travel to major entertainment destinations, such as Orlando and Las Vegas, will be seriously stalled while more Americans go someplace closer and cheaper—like into their living rooms to watch TV.

Businesses that survive during these leaner days will include low-end restaurants, low-end clothing stores, discount shops of every description, used clothing and household furnishing stores, and businesses that cater to local, inexpensive travel.

If you own a business in the Discretionary Spending Sector, you might want to give some very serious thought to selling your business now or in the next couple of years. Depending on what you sell and to whom you sell it, you may be able to survive. But only the most clever, well-placed, or just plain lucky businesses in this sector will truly thrive in the coming Bubblequake.

If you are currently employed in the Discretionary Spending Sector and are in a position to retrain for another career, now might be a very good time to start looking elsewhere, such as the Necessities Sector.

Some Good News: Cashing in on the Necessities Sector (Healthcare, Food, Basic Clothing, Transportation, Education, and Government Services)

Here's something that may help dry your tears: There is still some money to be made in the third area of the U.S. economy, the Necessities Sector, as well as some huge potential profits in another unexpected growth area we will tell you about in a moment.

The Necessities Sector of the economy, which is composed primarily of healthcare, education and government services, is primarily run by government or other nonprofit entities that don't pay too well. However, the private companies that supply these government and nonprofit entities have the potential to do quite well during the coming Bubblequake.

Of course, as things get increasingly negative for the rest of the economy, government spending on services and education will also decline. But for those who can find and keep a government job, and for those who either work for or own private businesses that provide goods and services within the Necessities Sector, you will likely survive.

Business Winners and Losers in the Necessities Sector

Healthcare is currently a very strong element of the U.S. economy and it will continue to be the best bet in the Necessities Sector after the bubbles pop, but not without some pain. Many people will lose their private medical insurance as they lose their jobs, which will initially cut into healthcare profits. The government will step in and fill the gap with Medicaid and Medicare, but benefits will be tight. With more and more aging Baby Boomers needing more and more healthcare, even when funding of benefits per capita goes down, overall demand for healthcare will continue to rise.

The loss of so many privately insured people will also cause some big losses for the healthcare industry, particularly in the area of healthcare capital goods, such as X-ray machines, CAT scanners, and hospital construction. However, businesses providing services and supplies to the healthcare industry will continue to do okay.

Another survivor will be most government services, with some notable exceptions. Surprisingly, government spending on the defense industry will take a very deep cut. It won't be because people all of a sudden don't care about defense, but when push comes to shove, and Americans have to choose between bombs and Band-Aids, they will reluctantly cut the Defense Department before pulling the plug on Medicare and Medicaid. Funding per capita on Medicare and Medicaid expenditures will decline, but before they make massive benefits cuts, we suspect they will drastically cut defense spending.

No one will like that decision, but the days when our government could simply borrow all the money needed to buy everything it wanted will be long gone. Deficit spending, at this point, is no longer an option. Paying down the deficit, primarily through massive inflation, will be forced on the government at the same time that it will be struggling to make ends meet because of a huge reduction in tax revenue. And let's not forget that the government won't be able to borrow money from Social Security taxes anymore because the surplus will be entirely gone. Currently, Social Security taxes fund more than a third of our deficit. Take that away and we are going to have huge government cuts in all areas, with defense spending near the top of the list.

Businesses and individuals who supply capital goods or construction services to the government will be hit. As new construction of both roads and buildings plummets, businesses that can make the switch to repair work and related sales will fare better.

Along with healthcare, the demand for public education will continue, so businesses that supply education or healthcare products or services to the government will benefit from strengthening their marketing and business ties to these areas and increasing their percentage of sales in these sectors.

Even within the relatively good Necessities Sector, if you are thinking about selling your business, sooner is better than later. If you are planning to sell your business in 5 to 10 years, strongly consider accelerating the time frame to 3 to 5 years, which will still give you plenty of time to improve and properly market your business.

Healthcare Could Become 25 Percent of the GDP When the Bubbles Pop

Healthcare will be one of the safest havens for business owners and workers in the Bubblequake. Currently, the huge healthcare industry accounts for about 16 percent of the nation's GDP. As other industries, especially in the Discretionary Spending and Capital Goods Sectors, decline, the relatively healthy healthcare industry will naturally assume a larger percentage of the economy. We've seen this on a smaller scale before, for example, during the oil bust in the 1980s, the percentage of the Houston, Texas, economy represented by nonoil industries grew dramatically.

Add to this an aging population with increasing demands for healthcare, and it is quite possible that healthcare could take over a staggering 25 percent of our economy after the bubbles pop.

That means, not only will the safest jobs and businesses be in healthcare during the Bubblequake, but also that the nation's hopes for regaining significant productivity growth in the post-bubble economy will most likely lie with dramatic productivity advancements in the healthcare field.

Finding the Best Jobs in the Necessities Sector

Needless to say, if you have to work for someone else, a Necessities Sector job is the place to be. Of course, jobs in this sector notoriously don't pay very well, and they will pay even less after the Bubblequake; but at least you will have a job, and it will be much more stable and reliable than any other job in the post-bubble economy.

Even at lower pay, Necessities Sector jobs will be a godsend for families with a spouse who used to make more money than his or her mate, but now is unemployed. The lower-paid, still-employed spouse, working as a nurse, teacher, medical administrator, or other Necessities Sector employee, will likely retain his or her job and be able to carry the family through the worst of the downturn.

Of these, healthcare jobs will be most likely to survive. That will include nurses, doctors, medical support personnel, administrative staff, and many others.

After healthcare, the next best positions in the Necessities Sector will be government services jobs, such as police and firefighters. Road construction and maintenance, as well as transportation in general, will do far worse. And education will also be hit hard as tax revenues drastically drop at both the state and local levels. Still, as a necessity, education jobs will hold up far better than jobs in the other areas.

Big Opportunities after the Bubbles Pop: Cashing in on Distressed Assets

In nearly every industry and in all three sectors of the economy, there will be many opportunities to benefit from the falling asset values. Just as high-priced office furniture from bankrupt dot-com companies ended up at yard sales for pennies on the dollar after the relatively small Internet Bubble popped, there will be countless irresistible bargains of every description up for grabs all over the planet after the biggest bubble crash the world has ever seen. Opportunities to make huge profits by buying and servicing distressed businesses and other assets will actually become an important growth area in our post-bubble economy.

As always, timing will be key. The most likely mistake people will make is buying distressed businesses too soon. In this very unusual economic downturn, involving the fall of multiple bubbles, we will face very high interest and inflation rates that will take a lot longer to bring down than anyone might imagine. It will be easy to mistakenly think the worst has passed and the time is right to start buying up distressed businesses and assets, when actually the price of these bargain properties will likely fall even lower. For maximum profits, think years not months.

For the most recent information on distressed asset timing, please see **www.americasbubbleeconomy.com/ distressedassets.**

In the meantime, the servicing of distressed assets and businesses will be an instant and long-term winner. Bankruptcy attorneys and auctioneers will obviously do quite well. So will a whole range of other people and companies that will buy, restructure, manage, and resell distressed businesses and other assets, making huge incomes and profits along the way. Among the winners will be:

- Attorneys and others in the legal industry, including those involved with bankruptcies, restructuring, foreclosures, etc.

- Accountants and others in the accounting industry, including those involved with forensic accounting and distressed properties accounting.

"I want my bubble back."

- Repair workers, particularly vehicle, road, and real estate repair.
- Consultants, bankers, managers, and others involved in the acquisition, restructuring, and management of distressed businesses and other assets.

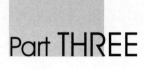

Part THREE

The Really <u>Big</u> "Big Picture"

Chapter EIGHT

The View from 30,000 Feet

Our Bubblequake Is Part
of a Much Broader Evolution

It may seem as if America's Bubble Economy arose entirely from near-term government decisions and recent economic trends, and in many ways this is true. But there's a lot more to this story than meets the eye, and if you have a few more moments to spend with us, we'd like to show you the rest of the picture now—both past and future. This final chapter won't help you protect assets, place investment bets, or find the best job when the bubbles finally pop, but when you make these vital decisions over the next years, you will have the satisfaction of knowing how we arrived at this unusual moment in time and some unique insights into where we could be headed next.

In any case, buckle your seatbelts. Whether you agree with our thinking or not, we promise you a very big Big Picture ride.

The View from 30,000 Feet: We Are Not Changing Randomly, We Are Evolving

If we could pull way back from this particular slice of time and view the bigger picture, the way an airplane flying high above the earth gives us a broader view of where we live, we would see a fascinating landscape that few people on the ground are talking about. At 30,000 feet, our current bubble economy and the coming Bubblequake can be seen, not merely as a collection of random events, isolated from the rest of time, but as a logical progression in a much broader trend—the evolution of our monetary system. We didn't just land in today's world by accident. Given our overall flight path, this was a logical—and to some extent, even predictable—place to end up.

By "predictable," we mean in the sense that the overall weather is predictable. While specific weather conditions at any one house vary based on many local, hard-to-predict factors, the overarching weather trend towards winter or towards summer goes beyond the random fluctuations at any one location. This is the same with our economy. The exact course of local financial events is always subject to many unpredictable forces, but the overall economic trend, like the trend toward summer or winter, is not random. It's part of a much larger evolution—the evolution of money itself.

This is the fundamental reason why the "economic cycles" argument only works for relatively narrow periods of time. Over the course of 100 years or more, and even as short as a few decades, economic cycles simply cannot fully explain how the economy changes. That's because we are *not* running in circles. *We are evolving.*

Understand this evolution and you can better understand how we got ourselves in our current bubble trouble and where we are likely headed next.

The Evolution of Money: From Barter to Barcodes

Many thousands of years ago, when the most basic trade between human beings first began, our monetary system was straight forward and simple: *You give me a chicken and I'll give you a basket of roots.* Barter was certainly direct, but not necessarily without complication: *If the chicken is big enough, you can keep the basket. But if the chicken is too skinny, I want the basket back, and you owe me one toad, which I'll pick up next week.* Sort of like a prehistoric version of *Let's Make a Deal.*

Strictly speaking, barter is really not a monetary system at all but a way for people to directly trade back and forth, one on one. Over time, as people traded more and more goods and services, back and forth, sometimes between large tribes, the barter system was made a bit easier with the use of standardized units: each item or service was assigned a value of so many cows, shells, or bushels of wheat, facilitating multiple trades like a big Stone Age eBay.

It's interesting to note that had we not evolved into bigger, more organized tribes, the barter system would not have been forced to evolve to accommodate the higher, most complex level of trade. As we will see shortly, the evolution of money has been driven forward by the even broader evolution of society itself—in a process we call *STEP Evolution.* More on that later. Right now, the point is that we developed a more organized form of barter,

219

involving shells and other objects so we could trade more effectively and efficiently with each other. In short, *barter evolved*. At first, we didn't need shells to make barter work; later we did. (see Figure 8.1).

Evolving from Barter to Money Based on Precious Metals

As time went by (many thousands of years), trade become even more complex. Why? Because we had more stuff to trade and more contact with people who wanted to trade, especially beginning about 4,000 BCE, when we figured out how to smelt metals into tools and other objects that made it possible to more efficiently build all sorts of things, like larger and more durable houses, weapons, and ships. As societies became more organized and complex, and as people wanted to trade more and more things, we naturally used the new technology of smelting metal to create something that would replace simple shells and other fragile barter trinkets with something more durable, easier to carry, and of more uniform value—metal coins, the world's first pocket change.

Metal coins fashioned out of gold, silver, copper, nickel, brass, and other metals have been used for many millennia. Over time, shiny silver and gold became the standout favorites, perhaps because we liked how they looked, and more importantly because they were quite rare (smaller supply, higher value), they had high value to weight, and they resisted rust and wear. Compared to using salt or wheat for money, metal money was far superior.

For larger transactions, the all time favorite has been gold. The value of a gold, silver, nickel, or any other metal

Figure 8.1 The Evolution of Money

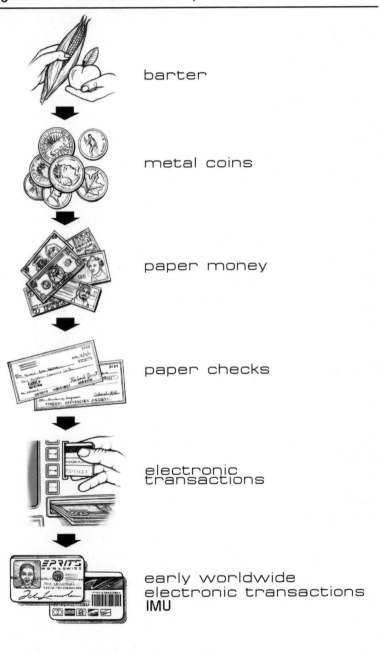

barter

metal coins

paper money

paper checks

electronic
transactions

early worldwide
electronic transactions
IMU

coin was simply set by the market price of that particular metal. A gold coin, therefore, was literally worth its weight in gold.

Gold (and to a lesser extent, silver) remained the metal money of choice as societies continued to evolve. After the movable type printing press in 1440 and the steam engine in 1769 ignited an explosion of trade around the world, more and more gold was needed to keep up with trade. After a while, great big bags of gold weighed too much to lug around all day, and large quantities of metal money were becoming too expensive to protect, transport, verify, and use. More importantly, there just wasn't enough gold available to keep up with so many transactions. By the 1800s in the United States, trade was simply growing too fast to dig up enough gold to keep pace with our rapidly expanding economy.

So, money was forced to evolve again.

Evolving from Metal Money to Paper Money

The solution was ingenious: create an IOU for gold or silver, and print it on lightweight paper. The limited supply of metal money was constrained by the rate in which gold and silver could be dug up out of the ground. On the other hand, paper money could easily be printed without the natural limitations of a gold or silver mine. Paper money was portable, foldable, and easy to conceal. Plus, unlike mining silver and gold, paper money was far less expensive to produce and protect.

But the biggest advantage of paper over metal money was even better than all that, because the ability to make and manage paper money gave the U.S. economy something it could really run with: room to rapidly grow. Paper money made it possible for the nation's money supply to more easily keep pace with expanding trade—but not without some problems.

A Run on the Bank

Today you'd get arrested for it, but back in the late 1800s, whenever private banks wanted more cash, they simply went in a back room and printed more dollars. To convince people this paper money was actually worth anything, banks guaranteed the value of their dollars by saying the paper money was "backed" by gold—meaning that for every paper dollar in circulation, there were actual piles of gold stashed away in bank vaults.

But bankers only had a limited amount of stashed gold, so instead of putting aside the full amount necessary to back every dollar they printed, they decided to set aside a certain percentage of the value of the dollars in gold. This is what economists called a "fractional reserve."

The idea that paper dollars were not 100 percent backed by gold naturally left some folks feeling a bit skittish about the true value of their paper cash, and so, not surprisingly, they weren't especially fond of using it. As late as 1890, many commercial transactions in the United States were still done with gold. And when Americans did use paper dollars, insecurity ran high. Every so often, panic would send people running to their banks to try to get back their money, creating what economists called "a run on the bank."

Backed by the Good Faith and Credit of the United States of America

Insecurity about the nation's currency was greatly reduced by the creation of the U.S. Federal Reserve in 1914. Instead of banks printing money, the government issued dollars "backed by the good faith and credit" of the United States. To prevent a run on a bank, the Fed could provide banks with additional dollars as needed, regulating the nation's money supply without causing panic.

The creation of the Fed and a national currency backed by the reputation and power of the federal government, not only put the public at ease, it helped dramatically increase domestic trade because there was enough money available for more and more financial transactions. The Fed's ability to increase and manage the nation's money supply, as needed, contributed significantly to the rapid growth of the U.S. economy in the roaring 1920s.

Taking the Metal Out of Money for Domestic Transactions Created Big Long-Term Gains, But Not Without Some Short-Term Pain

Evolving from metal money (gold) to paper money (dollars), and managing that paper money at a federal level, turned out to be a very powerful a tool for building national wealth.

Unfortunately, the newly established Federal Reserve failed to understand just how powerful a tool it had. After the 1929 stock market crash, the relatively inexperienced Fed did not know how to properly manage the nation's money supply well enough to prevent or cope with the Great Depression.

With the economy temporarily struggling and the nation needing more dollars than we had in available gold, President Franklin Roosevelt decided in the 1930s to free the Federal Reserve from the requirement to back paper money with piles of physical gold, and the dollar's evolution off the "gold standard" was complete. Instead of metal-based money, the country would benefit from the freedom of using dollars backed by the good faith and credit of the United States. Instead, our word would be considered as good as gold.

In the long run, after the short-term pain of the Depression, taking the metal out of money for domestic transactions allowed the U.S. economy to grow enormously in the 20th century. For more information, see **www.americasbubbleeconomy.com/depression.**

Taking the Metal Out of Money for International Transactions

Although we were no longer constrained by gold for domestic transactions, it took us another 40 years to drop gold from our international transactions, as well.

Prior to 1973, the value of the dollar overseas was determined by a fixed exchange rate and backed by gold. But after a while, we just didn't have enough gold available to back every dollar we wanted to trade. So in 1973, the only way the United States could continue to buy goods from foreign countries was to move off the gold standard for international transactions. Taking the metal out of money for international transactions meant the U.S. government no longer set the dollar at a fixed price, convertible into gold. Instead of the price of gold, the forces of supply and demand were allowed to determine the value of the dollar, with moderating control by central banks. No longer constrained by our limited gold reserves, our international trade was free to expand tremendously.

Essentially, we did for foreign trade in 1973 the same thing that we did for domestic trade earlier in the century. And, similarly, this move off the gold standard for foreign transactions was one of the reasons for the tremendous boom in foreign trade over the last 30 years.

Taking the Metal Out of Money for International Transactions Created Long-Term Gains, But Not Without Some Short-Term Pain

Just as going off gold for domestic transactions created long-term gains but also some short-term pain, going off gold for international transactions has and will continue to produce long-term gains—but not without the short-term pain of massive trade deficits and related temporary bubbles.

Going off of gold for foreign trade is like giving a college kid a credit card with a multi-trillion dollar credit limit. It can easily be misused. In the past, if you ran a trade deficit, you would eventually run out of gold and could trade no more. Today, freed from the constraint of running out of gold, we can run huge trade deficits—at least, for a while.

With so much freedom to spend and spend, it's no surprise that we began buying much more than we were selling, creating a massive International Trade Deficit Bubble. Importing more goods than we export means huge amounts of dollars flowing out. Once these dollars are in the hands of business people in other countries, many of these investors like to use their dollars to buy U.S. stocks, bonds, and real estate, hugely increasing the amount of foreign capital invested in the United States. As long as there are profits to be made, foreign investors will continue to buy, invest and loan dollars.

As we explained in Chapter Two, if investor psychology begins to sour and profit expectations start to evaporate—perhaps due to a significant stock market downturn or an unfavorable exchange rate—foreign investors will begin selling off their U.S. dollars, stocks, bonds, and other assets faster than a bookstore trying to unload last year's calendars.

At first, central banks will buy our dollars to stabilize its value. But such efforts can only go so far. Once the value of the dollar on the foreign exchange markets begins to slip enough that significant profits can be made in other currencies, the Dollar Bubble will crash, and nothing will stop the mad dash of foreign capital out of the United States.

It will be reminiscent, on an international level, of an old-fashioned run on the bank—for a while everyone will want their money back.

Unlike a run on the bank, however, no government will be able to stop it. A bank can be temporarily closed until people calm down. But no government will be able to stop investors all around the world from selling their U.S. stocks, bonds, real estate, dollars and other U.S. assets to whomever they wish for whatever price they can get. When there are more sellers than there are buyers, the selling price will drop, looking for a buyer.

The Short-Term Pain: Bubblequake

As we discussed in Chapter Two, with foreign investors dashing to get their capital out of their U.S. assets by selling them as fast as possible, the value of these assets will crash and our multiple bubbles will collide and fall. Our Dollar Bubble will become a greatly diminished dollar with far less buying power than it has today. The Stock Market Bubble will fall. The Real Estate Bubble will be but a distant memory. And the nation's astronomical $8 trillion Government Debt Bubble will suddenly become as hard to pay down as an interest-only mortgage on a giant McMansion for a family living on a McDonald's pay check.

Interest rates will climb, as will inflation. Unemployment will temporarily rise and consumer spending will be way down, including business and consumer spending on imports. The economies of other countries, especially those heavily dependent on exports, will falter. And the world's economy will be reeling with the temporary pain of a global Bubblequake recession.

The Short-Term Solution: Adam Smith's "Invisible Hand" Smackdown

The combined problem of imbalanced international trade and an overvalued dollar is very easy to solve—in the short run—with the normal free-market economics of supply and demand. The bursting of the Dollar Bubble is key. When China and Japan are no longer able to support the dollar and foreign investors begin losing lots of money on their dollar investments, the value of the dollar will fall to the point that imported goods are simply too expensive for Americans to buy.

That means, as the buying power of the dollar falls, at some point, the cost of a Toyota, for example, will be so high that people will prefer to buy GM and Ford cars. That price point may be $50,000 or it may be $100,000. Whatever the price point that stops Americans from buying imported cars, will be the top price for these cars, in dollar terms.

This is Adam Smith's "Invisible Hand" of supply and demand at work, automatically restoring balance to international trade by making it too expensive for us to import much from other countries. The Invisible Hand will guide the dollar to the proper level to stop imports and rebalance our foreign trade, popping our Trade Deficit Bubble and providing the bottom point for the falling Dollar Bubble.

Clearly, this automatic supply-and-demand solution solves the problem of imbalanced trade, but it is not a long-term solution because it severely damages world trade. Long-term, many changes will have to be made to revive world trade, including some dramatic changes in our international monetary system. Long-term improvements for the U.S. economy will include a rise in real wages, which haven't changed much in recent years (see Figure 8.2), as well as a significant boost to our productivity growth rate out of its current slump (see Figure 8.3).

Slowing Productivity Growth: The Real Trouble Behind the Bubble

When our bubbles collide and pop, the real trouble hiding behind America's Bubble Economy will get a whole lot harder to ignore: slowing productivity growth.

Figure 8.2 Real Wage Growth

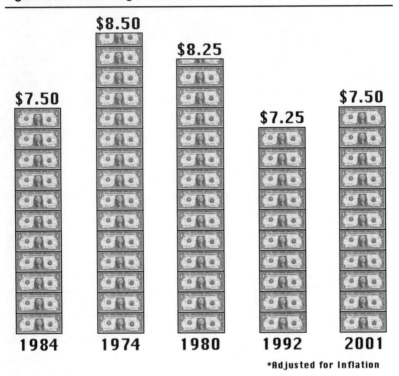

When adjusted for inflation, wages have failed to grow significantly for more than three decades.

Many influential economists insist that U.S. productivity grew dramatically during the late 1990's due to heavy investment in information technology. Other economists, such as Robert Gordon and Nobel Prize winner Robert Solow, say that overall productivity has been growing, but at a much slower rate since the mid-1970s, and the only reason people keep missing this fact is because productivity measurements ignore many key factors that impact real growth.

Figure 8.3 Slowing Productivity Growth

Although US productivity continues to grow, the rate of that growth has declined dramatically since 1970.

Please understand that when we use the term "productivity growth," we are not talking about the conventional output-per-man-hour statistics that go up and down with every monthly economic report. Beyond this narrow measure, we are talking about the really big picture of productivity growth that has driven the overarching rise of human efficiency and production over centuries—for example, reducing the number of people required to grow our food from 75 percent to just 3 percent of the nation's population because of advances in farming technology.

How to measure productivity growth is a tricky question that will continue to be debated for years. But,

231

from a Big Picture perspective, this much is clear: the dramatic productivity growth of the first half of the 20th century has fizzled out since the 1970s.

How do we know that? We know that because if productivity had grown significantly, so would have inflation-adjusted wages. In fact, real wages have grown very little in the last three decades (see Figure 8.2).

We used to have wonderful, prosperity creating productivity growth in the United States. From 1913 to 1972, our productivity grew at an average rate of 1.6 percent per year. That may not sound like much, but it was enough to make the United States the wealthiest nation on earth.

But by the 1970s, productivity growth in the U.S. and other advanced economies began to look as flabby as a Macy's Thanksgiving Parade balloon after the air has started to leak. Over the years, it's become increasingly difficult to significantly boost productivity simply by building bigger factories or using more machines. Other than the productivity improvements created by high-tech electronics, no other technology or industry has improved enough to drive significant productivity growth since the 1970s (see Figure 8.3).

You can easily spot this trend by looking at the growth of real wages: after adjusting for inflation, wages have failed to grow much since 1970. If productivity growth was significantly increasing over the last 30 years, we'd certainly see wages going up, too.

To get a feel for how productivity growth has leveled off, consider the flight pattern of the airline history. From 1900 to 1957, we went from not being able to fly at all to producing the powerful Boeing 707—quite an accomplishment. A half-century later, from 1957 to today, we have only managed to go from the 707 to the 777. That means, in the first half of the 20th century, aviation achieved the productivity equivalent of going from the runway to 30,000 feet; but in the second half of the 20th century, we've just inched up a bit higher.

With the exception of information technology, nearly every U.S. industry, from lumbering to farming to oil refining, has followed the same flight path: huge productivity gains during the first half of the 20th century, followed by much less dramatic productivity gains in the second half of the 20th century.

In the 1980s and '90s, personal computers and the Internet may have seemed like the Next Big Thing. But the actual productivity growth they created pales in comparison to the earlier productivity explosions ignited by the development of the internal combustion engine, electricity, telephones, and economies of scale in production. In truth, after the mid-1980s, productivity gains from investment in information technology came primarily from declines in the prices of personal computers and related equipment.

Meanwhile, the productivity superstars of yesteryear, while still driving some current productivity growth, are beginning to run out of steam:

- *In our factories,* assembly-line technologies and automated production of everything from mass-produced cars to machine-wrapped candy bars drove huge productivity improvements from 1910 to 1970. But other than some fine-tuning, there have been no equally dramatic productivity improvements since.

- *Down on the farm,* as we swapped work animals, wheel barrows and hand tools for tractors, trucks and fertilizers, food production skyrocketed from 1900 to 1970. But there hasn't been anything approaching that level of growth in the last 30 years.

  Nevertheless, many people continue to insist that productivity growth is still going strong. Some say that the Industrial Age has given way to the Information Age. But to fantasize that the modest productivity improvements created by the Internet, or even the significant improvements created by high-tech electronics, are in the same league as the truly massive productivity explosion propelled by electricity, airplanes, telephones, powerful steam engines, internal combustion engines, electric motors, freshly laid railroads, and new steel mills is like comparing a couple of fancy bicycles to a fleet of bulldozers.

  Yes, the Internet has had a significant impact on the productivity of some individuals and industries. (It sure made writing this book a lot easier.) But in our high-tech excitement, let's not lose track of the really Big Picture. Yes, our nation's productivity is still growing, but the rate of that productivity growth is slowing down.

How Will We Solve These Problems in the Long-Term?

We agree with the late Israeli diplomat and politician, Abba Eban, who said, "History teaches us that men and nations behave wisely once they have exhausted all other alternatives."

Eventually, we will solve our current monetary problems the same way human beings have been forced to solve every other major monetary problem since the beginning of time—evolution!

With domestic trade, we evolved from money based on metal to a monetary system governed by the Federal Reserve, which allowed more sophisticated control over the domestic monetary system that helped create the rapidly expanding domestic economy of the 20th century.

For international trade, the evolutionary pattern will be basically the same: We will go from foreign trade based on gold to a monetary system governed by an international equivalent of the Federal Reserve, which will create more sophisticated international monetary system that will help rapidly expand world trade. (We will tell you more about this in a moment.)

With domestic trade, evolving from gold to paper money turned out to be a good thing for growing the U.S. economy, but the transition was messy and helped create the Depression. Likewise, evolving from gold to paper money for international trade will also eventually lead to more wealth for the entire world, but the transition will be messy, and will help create the coming Bubblequake.

Bubblequake pain will provide the necessary pressure on governments to evolve and make the changes needed to create a much better global monetary system, the next step in the evolution of money. As always, the pain of not evolving provides the impetus to move forward. As in our own individual lives, it sometimes takes a short-term crisis to force us to move ahead. For more information, see **www .americasbubbleeconomy.com/moneyevolution.**

How Will Our Future Money Evolve?

No one knows for sure, but based on how things have gone so far, we think we have a clue. More than merely an educated guess, we think we know some general features of how money will evolve next because, as we said earlier, the evolution of money does not happen in a vacuum, but is actually part of a much broader evolution of society.

We call it STEP Evolution.

What follows is a *basic introduction* to STEP Evolution—a powerful and reliable new way of understanding how things non-randomly change, which we look forward to telling you a lot more about in another book. For now, here are the very basics. Love it or hate it, please let us know what you think about STEP Evolution and how the coming Bubblequake fits into it by visiting us at **www.americasbubbleeconomy.com/STEP**

Introducing the Biggest "Big Picture" on the Block: STEP Evolution

American song writer Woody Guthrie once said, "Any fool can make something complex; it takes a genius to make something simple."

Simplicity is our goal.

Just as we have a theory of *physical evolution* that helps explain how matter started with the Big Bang and evolved into our universe, and we have a theory of *biological evolution* that helps explain how living things evolved after the Big Bang, it is possible to imagine that a theory of *societal evolution* might help explain how human society has evolved (after a great deal of biological evolution) and how it may continue to evolve into the future.

Stated in the most simple terms, **S-T-E-P Evolution** is the co-evolution of **S**cience, **T**echnology, **E**conomics, and **P**olitics.

From the beginning of human history and continuing into our shared future, Science, Technology, Economics, and Politics are not simply changing randomly through time, but are inevitably linked and evolving together. At any moment in time—past, present, or future—each depends on the others, and each changes in response to the others.

In other words, it's a package deal.

That's why we didn't have cell phones in the Middle Ages when the science, economics, and politics of the day simply could not have produced that technology. That's why important advancements in science—like the idea the world is round—simply will not be accepted until the supporting technology, economics, and politics evolves enough to handle them. And that's why once powerful kings will inevitably fade from world politics when the prevailing winds of science, technology, and economics change.

Throughout time, science, technology, economics, and politics have been linked and coevolving together. In fact, each pushes the others forward: Science drives technology, technology changes economics, and economics shapes politics:

Science → **T**echnology → **E**conomics → **P**olitics

Science Ultimately Drives Social Change

At first blush, such a statement may seem unlikely. But when we look at the evidence over thousands of years, a clear pattern emerges. Science—that is, our collective knowledge about the world—is the driving force behind the evolution of human society. We don't say this because we love science and we want it to be true. We say it because that is what the evidence shows.

You can see this for yourself by breaking STEP Evolution down into . . . well, steps.

The first step in STEP Evolution is undeniable: Science (our collective knowledge about the world) drives technology. You can't have TV (a technology) without knowing something about electricity and many other types of knowledge (science). So it seems perfectly plausible to say that changes in science drive changes in technology.

<u>S</u>cience → <u>T</u>echnology

Throughout history, advancements in <u>S</u>cience have driven the development of new <u>T</u>echnology. That's how we figured out how to make sharp metal arrowheads and tools, instead of relying on sharpened rocks tied to sticks. Clearly, over the years, advances in science have given us all sorts of useful innovations—things like antibiotics, instant coffee, Velcro, and computers. Of course, not all new technologies are created equal; some are more helpful than others.

But here's where it gets interesting and perhaps unexpected. These new technologies aren't just interesting gadgets and inventions. They have profound effects on our lives. From the beginning of human history, new technologies have vastly transformed how we live and compete for survival, changing everything from what we eat to how we trade goods and services.

In other words, new Technologies profoundly affect Economics.

Think of the dramatic economic changes that followed the invention of the steam engine or the printing press, for example. How in the world would we ever have developed an industrial economy without first having industrial technology? It just wouldn't happen. Technology changes and that forces economics to change.

Technology → Economics

Sure, there are countless relatively small changes in the economy that have little to do with new technology, but that's not what we are talking about. Think *big* Big Picture. How far would global trade (economics) have advanced without bigger, steam-powered ships (technology) that could cross an ocean? But once we have those ships, how in the world could we have stopped global trade from eventually evolving? On a big scale, new technology forces economics to change.

And it doesn't stop there. In time, sweeping new Economic conditions inevitably reshape Politics—including how people share resources and power, fight wars, follow or defeat leaders, and run governments.

Economics → Politics

This means, when economics significantly changes, so too do our political structures. In fact, you can't stop Politics from changing once Economics changes—eventually, the new economic conditions topple the old system and help support a new system. That's why we don't have too many monarchies left in highly prosperous nations with large middle class populations. That kind of economy just doesn't support kings and queens as nicely as previous economies did.

So, if science drives technology, and technology changes economics, and economics inevitably reshapes politics, then it is reasonable to say that science (our collective knowledge about the world) is driving societal change.

<u>S</u>cience → <u>T</u>echnology → <u>E</u>conomics → <u>P</u>olitics

In short, science drives new technology, which gives us new ways to compete for survival, which reshapes

"Sir, the following paradigm shifts occurred while you were out."

economics, which transforms politics, and over time, ultimately drives our evolving world.

Therefore, if science (our collective knowledge of the world) is changing non-randomly and is building on itself and evolving, then everything else is evolving, too.

But Isn't Our World Changing Randomly?

No, not if you look at the truly *big* Big Picture. Certainly, lots of things do come and go randomly through time. But over the course of thousands of years, the big general features of human society have evolved non-randomly.

This makes sense. Given that advancements in science systematically build on each other, and given that new technologies don't simply materialize out of the blue, it follows that human society—when viewed over the broad sweep of time—is also changing non-randomly, building on what came before, following an evolutionary path.

As Isaac Newton once said, when referring to his dependency on Galileo's and Kepler's work in physics and astronomy, "If I have seen further, it is by standing upon the shoulders of giants."

Of course, countless fits and starts take place, but over the long haul of history, science (our collective knowledge about the world) advances systematically. Therefore, technology, when viewed over the long haul of history, advances systematically. Economics—which only changes significantly when it has to change because of new technology—also advances systematically. And our political structures, which only change dramatically when forced to change by new economic conditions, also advances systematically.

Science, technology, economics, and politics—in other words, the basic elements of human society—evolve!

It may seem as if things are changing randomly, but if you stand far enough back and take a big enough view, we can see that a certain amount of evolutionary progress has been made. While life on planet earth is far from perfect, over the centuries, STEP Evolution has worked in our favor. We may occasionally feel nostalgic for bygone days, but do we really want to live without plumbing, have to kill what we eat with our bare hands, and perhaps die at the ripe old age of 27 from a rotten tooth because we have no antibiotics? On the whole, STEP Evolution has worked to ease our struggles to survive and prosper, greatly increasing our productivity, health, and quality of life.

Now, here's where it gets really fun. History does not repeat itself, but the forces that shape history do. If we can figure out how the forces of STEP Evolution changed the past into the present, we can begin to understand how the present may evolve into the future. Why? Because the same forces that propelled the past to evolve into today, will continue to drive the present to evolve into tomorrow. Understand these forces and you can have some clue about what may happen next.

Come on, Can We REALLY Predict Future Social Evolution?

Of course, we cannot predict the details of the future, but we most certainly can predict that the future will *evolve*. And based on what we know about that evolution, we can even venture a general guess about what that the future might look like.

242

Predicting the general features of the future with STEP Evolution is sort of like trying to figure out the general features of an unknown object—say, a dinosaur—when all we have to work with are the most basic building blocks, the fossilized bones. When trying to reconstruct a dinosaur, we will never figure it all out, down to the tiniest detail. But if we know what we're looking at, bones can tell us a lot. By putting the pieces together and applying what we know about other living creatures, we can get a pretty good picture of something no human has ever seen. True, we won't know what a dinosaur thought about or what it ate for lunch on a specific day. But with enough bones and enough science, we can confidently predict it had a long tail, big jaws, and a relatively small brain. And although we'll never get to see it in action, we can predict, based on the science of how other animals move, that it probably ran like the wind. In this way, we can use the basic bones of evidence of how STEP Evolution has changed the world so far to construct our best guess about how the world will evolve next. Again, we are not trying to predict the details of the future; we are predicting future evolution.

This requires that we ignore many distracting details and stand way back to get a very broad view of what has already occurred. Just as you can't stare at a mountain and watch it evolve, you can't see STEP Evolution by focusing only on today or the recent past. STEP Evolution is the evolution of science, technology, economics, and politics over very broad sweeps of time—not a few years or even a few decades. Just as the earth is the product of billions of years of geological evolution, human society is the culmination of thousands of years of STEP Evolution. And as long as the sun continues to shine, our future will be the continuation of it.

Sounds Interesting, But What Good Is STEP Evolution to Us Today?

Plenty. In the short term, we can use STEP Evolution to help predict emerging trends in technology and business over the next 10 to 20 years. We look forward to telling you much more about this in another book, but right now, it's important you understand that STEP Evolution is not just an interesting way to think about life, but also a highly practical and powerful tool with many, many specific applications in business, technology, personal finances, and social and economic trends.

For example, STEP Evolution tells us what specific signs to watch for as we head into the coming Bubble-quake. In the near-term, it points us in the direction of the best jobs and hottest careers just on the horizon. And it offers detailed advice on how to invest wisely and protect your assets throughout the changing times ahead, some of which we shared with you in earlier chapters.

Well beyond the scope of this book, STEP Evolution and it's many tools can help shed light on how specific industries, technologies, and business sectors will fair in the near future. It can even help make specific, very practical recommendations to individuals and companies. (For more information on how STEP Evolution can be used for very practical, present-day purposes, go to **www .americasbubbleeconomy.com/STEP**.)

Taking the long-term view, STEP Evolution helps illuminate the bigger picture of where we've been and where we're going next, putting today's headlines into the much broader context of big, evolving change. Knowing how the past evolved into the present, and how the present continues to evolve into the future, offers tremendous insights into today's world. Present-day problems like poverty, crime, racism, terrorism, and wars cannot be fully understood, nor effectively solved, until we understand how they evolved in the first place.

Rather than pushing any particular social reform or political agenda, STEP Evolution objectively analyzes the key forces that have shaped history to better explain where we are today and where we're likely to go tomorrow. For more information see **www.americasbubbleeconomy.com/ STEP.**

What Does All This Have To Do With the Future of Money?

Everything. Although we have left this introduction to STEP Evolution to the end of the book, we have actually been using it all along. STEP Evolution and its many powerful tools can be used to analyze *any* type of big societal change, including the future of money. STEP Evolution can even analyze how a significant event—like the coming Bubblequake—fits into the larger evolution of money and the even broader evolution of science, technology, economics, and politics.

If you doubt that the general future of money (or the general future of anything) is in any way predictable, please remember what we said at the start of this chapter. By "predictable," we mean in the sense that a general weather trend is predictable. The exact course of specific, local events is always subject to many unpredictable forces, but the overall trend (like the overarching trend toward summer or winter) is to a certain extent predictable and not entirely random.

Again, we will leave the specific details about STEP Evolution and it's many tools to another book. For now, here's how the evolution of money—including the coming Bubblequake—fits into STEP Evolution, and what it means for the future of the international monetary system.

The Future of Money: How Bubblequake Will Drive A Messy Transition to a Long-term International Solution

So far, we have seen that money has evolved from simple barter to complex barter, and then to metals-based money (mostly gold and silver). We also saw that the evolution from metals-based money to paper money has given us many advantages—but not without some short-term pain. That's because evolution, as it is occurring, is not perfect. Evolution is messy. It goes through difficult periods of transition, just as a child becoming an adult must suffer through being a teenager. Transitions are always messy and often painful. Evolution involves short-term pain for long-term gain.

For example, moving off metal-based money for domestic transactions (U.S. dollars no longer backed by gold) allowed the Federal Reserve to print as much money as it needed to keep up with the expanding U.S. economy, but the bumpy, messy transition included the Great Depression.

Likewise, the evolution of moving off metal-based money for international transactions (U.S. dollars overseas no longer backed by gold) will also help expand the world's economy, but the bumpy, messy transition will include the coming Bubblequake. America's Bubble Economy and the world's current dependence on it are all part of the bumpy, messy transition in the evolution of money from metals-based money to something entirely different—not paper money, but the next step in the STEP Evolution of Money: an international all-electronic currency.

Okay, before you slam the book shut and tell all your friends we are trying to promote some whacky one-world agenda, hold on and let us explain.

First of all, this isn't going to happen any time soon, probably not in our lifetimes or even in our children's life times because the resistance to it will be fierce. The truth is—like every other step in our evolution—we wouldn't even dream of doing it unless we absolutely had to. And eventually, we will absolutely have to, thanks to the coming Bubblequake.

After many years of painful Bubblequake, the current reality of so many countries, each with their own paper currencies that have more or less evolved away from metals, is going to become increasingly untenable. Problems with the exchange of currencies, which cause instabilities in the value of the world's collective money, will have to be solved in order for the world economy to recover and expand.

Just as people eventually had to replace barter with more useful metal coins, and then metals-based money had to be eventually replaced with more useful paper money, the next step is to replace paper money with something more functional and less problematic. Driven forward through time by STEP Evolution, the next step in the evolution of money will be the development of an international agency (the global equivalent of an international central bank), managing a single international currency that is entirely electronic. As we already said, this will not come quickly nor easily, but eventually it will come. In time, old-fashioned cash stashed under the mattress will become as obsolete as a manual typewriter.

Why a Single International Currency?

Because it will be necessary to avoid repeating the pain of another global Bubblequake. A single international currency will eliminate the problems with foreign currency exchange, making currency bubbles (like our current Dollar Bubble) impossible. It will also block us from spending our way into huge foreign trade imbalances (like our current International Trade Deficit Bubble). And, because a single international currency is the most technologically and economically efficient form of money at this stage of our societal evolution, it will eventually become the best option.

Will nations resist it every inch of the way? Absolutely . . . for a while. But eventually, they will come around, for the same reasons evolution always occurs: because it beats the alternative. In the long view of STEP Evolution, a global economy requires a global currency.

Why an Electronic Currency?

Because money—like every other human technology since the Stone Age—evolves through time following the STEP Evolution principles of "Material Substitution" and "Energy

Substitution," which we will tell you more about in the STEP Evolution book. For now, all you need to know is that electronic technology will eventually be the next step in money.

Certainly, we have the beginnings of an electronic money system already in place. Credit cards, debit cards, electronic checks, checks by phone, checks by fax, direct deposit, and on-line banking and bill paying are all beginning to supplant some of our cash and check payments. Why? Because they are so much more efficient. Moving cash around in a big, money bucket brigade is expensive, requiring banks, ATMs, armored cars and security personnel. The cost of cash maintenance and cash crimes drains a society's productivity.

Remember those big bags of gold coins we don't bother lugging around anymore? Remember the high cost of mining, protecting, and using gold? Sooner or later, people do prefer cheaper, easier, and better—especially when the consequences of not evolving become very, very painful, as they will in the coming Bubblequake.

Hard To Believe? Actually, We're Already on Our Way

It may be hard to believe we will ever have a single international currency, given how fond individual nations are of their own currencies. But when you look at how far we've already come, it's easier to see that we're much more than half way there now.

Imagine how hard it would have been, 2,000 years ago, to convince hordes of Germanic tribal chiefs, wrapped in bear skins, that their warring tribes of 10,000 or more people would eventually come together to form a single European Union in the 20th century, with a single European currency, the euro. Given how far we've already come, it's only a matter of time before Japan, the United States, and the European Community come together, too, to create a common international currency.

Again, we are not saying this because that is what we hope will happen. This is not about wishful thinking or pushing some political agenda. In the big picture of STEP Evolution, evolving to a single electronic currency is just a matter of time. Sooner or later, unless the sun fails to shine or we blow up the planet, all other less efficient options will simply be eliminated.

A Likely Scenario for How Our New International Currency Will Evolve

The natural solution to the coming global Bubblequake will feel as unnatural to many Americans as giving up baseball. But sooner or later, major social and political changes, including a single, global electronic currency, operated by a central administrative agency, are in the cards for us. After the global Bubblequake recession, an international electronic currency, operated by a central administrative agency, will eliminate foreign exchange problems. We don't know what this new currency will be named, but for convenience, let's call it *imu* (pronounced eye-mew), short for International Monetary Unit.

Remember, this is not going to happen next week. First the bubbles have to pop, next we have to go through several years of Bubblequake and post-Bubblequake recovery, and then, eventually, we will evolve.

At first, the imu will simply be a merger of the euro,

the dollar, and the yen. The Asian Rimlands may first form their own "Asian euro." Eventually, as China becomes more democratic, it, too, will join the Asian euro and then the imu. Russia will join, too, either by adopting the euro, or changing directly to the imu.

Imus will be far cheaper for society to administer than cash. There'll be no expensive bills to print or coins to mint. There'll be no cash to steal. Imus will be inflation-free because the system that controls the supply of imus will be set up to avoid it. For more information on the imu and its adoption, see **www.americasbubbleeconomy.com/imu.**

Many people, including some Americans, will oppose the coming evolutionary transition to a new form of money; but change is inevitable. When America's Bubble Economy pops, and people ride the roller coaster from denial to panic to anger to understanding, the first thing they'll do is blame the politicians. Of course, it will be too late to punish the politicians who created and maintained the problem over many decades, but we will, no doubt, punish whomever we can.

Congress and the White House will become a revolving door as the party out of power blames the party in power for the country's economic woes. Government will be unable to solve the problem, at least not for a while, and each election will bring in new blood. This may be a good time for women and minorities in office, since anyone not in power at the time of the crash will have a shot at moving in to try to change things. Change can happen in a number of ways. A wise, courageous, but politically suicidal president could sacrifice his party's power by instituting radical reform. The same thing could happen today if a president chose to burst the bubble early to lessen our fall.

But the possibility that any president would willingly devalue the dollar or purposely shrink stock prices is about as unlikely as the lion king, having clawed his way to the top of the food chain, suddenly going vegetarian. The political system's own Darwinian process selects against leaders who harm their party's chances in the next election.

What's far more likely is that nothing will change in the next few years. Then the Bubblequake will hit, the president will get the boot and so will whoever comes in next. The revolving doors in Washington will scare off competent politicians and attract the most radical elements of both parties.

Eventually, after we've endured the political version of *The Beverly Hillbillies* for several election cycles, candidates will step forward who are willing to support real and responsible reforms, politicians more like Franklin Roosevelt than Herbert Hoover.

To do so, they'll have to cross political boundaries that haven't been crossed since the New Deal when FDR pushed through a number of interventionist government agencies like the Social Security Administration, the Securities and Exchange Commission, the Federal Deposit Insurance Corporation, and welfare. Whether you think FDR saved the country with deposit insurance or saddled it with expensive poverty programs, you have to admit he did force politicians of all stripes to confront the problems of the day and come up with ways to deal with them.

Evolutionary changes won't come overnight but, like mice in a maze, we are going to run down every avenue until we eventually solve our problems. When the dust finally settles, the result of this financial crisis will be sweeping political and economic changes, including a far more stable money system and much higher incomes for the entire world.

As long as nations continue to cling to their own currencies, we will face potential difficulties in how those currencies are valued in relation to each other. Problems with foreign exchange didn't exist before we evolved enough to have so much global trade. Now that we have global trade, we need a global currency. Until we have it, we will have problems—like our coming painful Bubblequake. Fortunately, pain is just the thing we need to help move this transition along.

In the meantime, like every other important societal change so far, our messy transition into the future will involve some resistance, followed by struggle, crisis, suffering, more struggle, and eventually, when all else fails . . . *evolution.*

Index